Picture, If You Will…

By

Richard R. Booth

ISBN: 0-7596-9028-6 (ebook)
ISBN: 0-7596-9029-4 (softcover)

This book is printed on acid free paper.

1stBooks – rev. 06/10/02

<u>*THE*</u> **HANDBOOK FOR ALL THOSE WHO WANT TO BE THE LIFE OF THE PARTY!**

PICTURE, IF YOU WILL…
BY
RICHARD R. BOOTH

CO-FOUNDER AND EXECUTIVE DIRECTOR OF
THE SOCIETY OF LOQUACIOUS VERBOSITIES

<u>ONE OF THE THREE OR FOUR BEST STORY-TELLERS</u>

EAST OF THE ROCKIES

ONE HUNDRED-FIFTY OF THE BEST STORIES

IN THE GALAXY,

MOST OF WHICH YOU'VE NEVER HEARD.

<u>THE</u> HANDBOOK FOR ALL THOSE

WHO WANT TO BE

THE LIFE OF THE PARTY.

<u>CROSS-INDEXED UNDER SUBJECT HEADINGS</u>

FOR READY REFERENCE.

* * * * * * * *

<u>DEDICATION</u>

This volume which is part of a collection
of anecdotes harking back
to 1949, and earlier, is dedicated
to my son, Richard Ross Booth, Jr.,
my daughter, Lynn Partridge Booth,
and my grandson, Spencer Ross Booth.

TABLE OF CONTENTS
References Are To Joke Numbers

ACKNOWLEDGEMENTS

I cannot help but acknowledge the following persons, many of whom, through cheerful and persistent nagging over a period of many years, finally overcame my static inertia and thereby contributed to the completion and publication of this singular volume, namely, viz and to wit: Baron Sepy Dobronyi, Archie Baldocchi, Al Shelby, Jim Sibley, John Mason, De Johnson, Bill Stephens, Will Dickens, Wahneta Sessions, the late Hugh Sowards, Mari Arnold, Al Smith, Michelle Headley, Hank Green, Dave Kraslow, Ingrid Savin, Don Jackson, Margret Ives, Jim Korth, Max Kuniansky, Bob Buck, Monty Young, Dave Hallstrand, Bob Rayon, and other friends at Royal Palm Tennis Club, Waverly Mueller, Dorrit Jensen, Mel Stier, Dick Perryman, Hal Barkas, Peggy Harum, the members of The Society of Loquacious Verbosities, my brother John, my sister Margo Piper, the late Russ Bramblet, the late Barney Buist, Stan Ordway and other surviving pilots of the 485th Fighter Squadron, and the respective spouses or significant others thereof and thereunto appertaining.

Back in June, 1949, I started taking notes on the jokes that people told me. The great majority of these were cocktail-party stories, in those days generally referred to as "dirty jokes".

I did this because I had learned from experience that when I heard a joke for the second time I remembered having heard it before, and, usually, the punch line, but…and this was what galvanized me into action…I found that I had not remembered the story well enough to call it to mind in sufficient detail to enable me to tell it to someone else. This, I find, is a common problem among those who strive to be dedicated raconteurs…or racontootsies.

So, what I did with respect to recording new stories as I heard them, was to immediately make notes, on anything available, consisting of essential clue words and the punch line. My notes were composed with such particularity as to enable me, in most cases, to type the story in full when I was able to access my typewriter. The next step was to tell the story a few times, with a personal touch perhaps, in such a manner as to eventually develop my reputation as one of the three or four best joke-tellers east of the Rockies.

After typing the story up and adding it to my growing file, I'd condense it to a clue line, assign a number and add it to my list. This master list was numbered serially as jokes were acquired, being typed with a pre-Xerox carbon copy. The original was placed in my file, and the carbon copy was on or near my person at all times when I was in a social situation. I became known for carrying this list around with me.

I have always made it a practice not to identify a joke on my list by the punch line, for reasons that must be obvious. If I were to show my list to a friend so that he or she might pick out a joke by the number assigned to it, it would ruin the telling of the joke if the punch line were to be prematurely exposed right there on my list.

More recently jokes have been flying wildly through cyberspace, somewhat willy-nilly; no one seems to know much about their authorship and although I am presently a non-possessor of a computer, friends frequently download such material and copy the same to me. Some of this is included in the second part of this book.

So much for the format of my notes and the list. Now to the reason for publishing this collection that has been growing for lo these many years, to wit: many friends for a magnitudinous numerousity of years have encouraged me to do just that. That's the simple answer, and of course it's somewhat of an ego trip to see a publication with one's name on it.

The stories appearing in this publication include many that you have not heard before. Some are stories that I have only heard once, because they are intricately worded or require a dialect or accent of some sort. I have found that few people will go to the trouble of memorizing a story that is intricately worded or will take the time to learn how to mimic, or simply can't manage, an accent or dialect. I feel sure that the reader will concede that a story loses a lot in the telling, or just falls flat, if the story-teller is unable to handle that aspect of the art.

The title of the book, PICTURE, IF YOU WILL…was selected advisedly. For years I have prefaced most stories I tell with that phrase, because it sets the stage for the audience. When you say it, their minds, respectively, immediately go blank and become receptive. They are ready to picture something; you have their attention. As the story progresses the listener tends to conjure up a picture of what is taking place in the telling, often ascribing personalities to the characters in the story, virtually viewing the prevailing circumstances and the activity inherent in the narrative on his or her cranial movie screen.

One distinguishing feature of this collection of anecdotes is the subject-matter cross-index. There are two; the first covers the first 150 stories appearing in the original book, and the second one covers the balance of 309 stories. This feature is for the ready reference of the reader who wants to put his finger on a story suitable to the circumstances of the moment.

Here then is PICTURE, IF YOU WILL… I hope you enjoy it and that it gives you the confidence to shine in the various social situations where humour is appropriate.

THE STAND-UP COMIC

1.

Picture, if you will...a comedy club; it's Thursday; open-mike night, and a guy has signed up to perform under the name 'John Smith'. His time comes and he is called to the stage. His routine is very clever, and he is a hit with the crowd. His act is hilarious, and people are rolling around the floor holding their sides. He wins first prize easily, and the proprietor of the club takes him aside and says, "You went over big tonight; come back tomorrow night and I'll give you a ten-minute spot. I want to see how you'll do with the usual Friday-night crowd."

The next night he is again a smash hit with those attending. The owner takes him aside and says, "Well, you did it again! I think you have a great career ahead of you as a stand-up comic. I'll give you thirteen weeks here in my club and see to it that you get gigs in a lot of other clubs around the country. We have a virtual network. But let me make a suggestion: 'John Smith' is no name for a comic." "Yeah, I know," says the comic, "I've been thinking about that too, and I've settled on a name; how do you like, 'Penis Van Lesbian'?" "You've got to be kidding; let's get serious," says the owner. "All right," replies the comic, "how about 'Dick Van Dyke?'"

CONFESSIONS

2.

Picture, if you will...a confessional booth in a small Catholic church in a medium-sized city in the Midwest. On this particular morning three married men in a row confess that they have been doing forbidden things with a hooker named 'Pussy Green'.

The following Sunday at 10:00 Mass a gorgeous and voluptuous blonde in a micro-miniskirt is sitting in the front row of the church crossing and uncrossing her long slender perfectly-formed legs from time to time.

The priest, who had heard the confessions and who is relatively new to the church turns to the acolyte who is lighting the candles and helping with communion, and says in a low voice, "Is that Pussy Green?" (indicating the young lady in question by discreetly pointing with his elbow.) To which the altar boy says, "No, I don't think so, I think that is just the way the light strikes it through the stained-glass window."

NUN OF THAT

3.

Picture, if you will...a nunnery. Each Thursday a priest comes to their premises to hear confessions. On one of these Thursdays a young pretty nun comes out of the room where the confessions are being taken and she has a particularly stilly grin on her face. This is observed by the Mother Superior who takes her aside and says, "Sister Angelique, come with me to my quarters, I think we should have a little talk." When they get there the Mother Superior says, "All right, young lady, I want to know what went on in that room today; you were in there quite a long time, and that needs explaining; and I want all the truth!"

The young nun sheepishly tells the MS what has occurred, "Well, a few months ago when I gave my first confession to the Father, he asked me if I wanted to go to heaven someday, and I said, 'Yes, Father, I do'. He then pulled up my habit and pulled down my panties, and, pointing to the place between my legs, he said that is the lock to the gates of heaven, and the way to open the lock and be sure that I would be going to heaven was to put his key in my lock. He then showed me his key which was jutting out from between his legs and showed me how the key fit the lock. He pleased me greatly, and every Thursday we have repeated the procedure to make sure that the key and the lock still fit each other."

The Mother Superior is shocked and says, "Why that crafty old bastard; he told me that it was Gabriel's horn, and I've been blowing it every week for the last thirty years!"

THE OBSESSION MAMMARIAL

4.

Picture, if you will…a suburban residential neighborhood, a cul-de-sac, nice homes. A moving van is in front of the house next door to a thirtyish young divorced guy. He notices that the people who are moving in are very attractive, and he is quick to notice that the wife, who is wearing a sweater and skirt, has the most beautiful breasts he has ever seen or could imagine. He becomes obsessed with the thought of seeing, fondling and kissing them.

Finally he approaches the husband of his obsession and says that he would pay $1,000 just to see her breasts uncovered. The man is surprised to say the least, but this has been a costly move and they could use the grand, so he says, "I'd have to run that by the wife; after all, it is her body we're talking about." Well, the wife agrees, so the next day they meet at the single guy's house at the appointed time, and she uncovers her breasts, and the guy goes crazy; he can't believe how perfect they are. He stares at them and practically drools. He says, "Another thousand if I can just fondle them." The couple agrees, and he proceeds to up and caress the exceptional orbs in question.

He can't stand it, and says, "$10,000, if I can kiss them and suck on the nipples!" The couple says why not – this is a real bonanza for them and for that price they can see no harm in giving him his wish. Whereupon, the guy takes one breast in each hand, kissing each nipple in turn, back and forth like a windshield wiper all the while saying, between kisses, "I don't know; I don't know, I don't know…"

After a few minutes of this, the husband says, "What's with all these 'I don't knows?'", To which the guy says, still oscillating back and forth one nipple to the other, "I don't know, I don't know, I just don't know…how I'm going to pay for this!"

IT DRIVES HER CRAZY

5.

Three guys are discussing what drives their respective wives crazy. The first says, "I come home from work with a bunch of roses; my wife is lying face up on the bed, naked of course. I take the petals from the flowers one by one and place them very carefully all over her body. Then I blow them off 'Poof!' one by one, very slowly. **IT DRIVES HER CRAZY!"**

The second says, "I come home from work; I have with me a can of Cool Whip. My wife is lying on the bed, naked and on her back. I shoot little puffs of Cool Whip all over her body, then I lick them off, one by one, very slowly. **IT DRIVES HER CRAZY!"**

The third man, a Georgia redneck, says, "Ah've got y'all beat on this one," he says, ah come home from work; ah throw mah wife on the bed and f k her brains out; then ah get up and wipe mah Johnson on the drapes. **IT DRIVES HER CRAZY!"**

DIPLOMACY

6.

Picture, if you will…the produce section of a supermarket. A man is examining the lettuce. He turns to an employee who is doing something with other vegetables and says, "This lettuce looks very nice; I'd like to buy half a head, please." The other replies, "I'm sorry sir, but we don't sell half heads of lettuce here." To which the man respond, "Well, would you mind asking your manager if you can sell me half a head?" The other says, "I'll go talk to him and if he says to sell you half a head I'll be pleased to do so." With this the store employee proceeds to go back to the manager's office and says, "Boss, you won't believe it; some nut case out in produce wants to buy a half a head of lettuce" And then noticing out of the corner of his eye that the customer had followed him back to the manager's office, with scarcely a pause he adds with a sweeping gesture, "And this gentleman would like the other half!"

PUNCTUALITY

7.

Two intellectual gentlemen meet frequently to discuss matters of cosmic importance. One is always found to be on the spot at the appointed time, and the other is habitually impunctual. One time, however, the latter is there when the other arrives. He says, "Ah! you're first at last; before you were behind, and I am pleased to see that you're early of late.

GO SOUTH, YOUNG MAN

8.

Picture, if you will…a young man who has just been told by his doctor that tests have revealed that he has AIDS. "Oh, my God," he says, "What can I do?" "Well, actually, not much," says the doctor, "but I have a suggestion: go to Mexico, deep into the a rural section where tourists are not likely to travel. Find a small agricultural community; go into the fields and eat all the lettuce you can stand, right out of the ground. When you get thirsty, go into the plaza…that's like a town square…you'll find a pipe coming out of a wall, and water will be flowing from the pipe. Drink all the water you can." "Will that help me, doctor?" asks the young man. "No, it won't," replies the doctor, "but it might teach you what your ass is for!"

WAS IT REAL?

9.

Picture, if you will…a man who has just made love to his wife. He says, "You faked it, didn't you?" She replies, "No! I really was asleep."

THE CREDIT REPORT

10.

A client asked me to get a credit report on a man who was pressing him for a loan. Two days later I received the credit report by fax; it read, "We have examined into the financial responsibility of the above-named person and find that he has no credit, either actual or potential; no property, either real or personal; no prospects, either present or future, and no hope either here or hereafter."

BETTER WRITE IT DOWN

11.

Picture, if you will…an elderly couple watching T-V. A Haagen-Daz commercial comes on picturing a hot fudge sundae with pecans on top. He says, "Boy, would I like one of those!" And she says, "Boy, me too!." He says, "I think I'll go down to the store and get one for each of us." She says, "Better write it down; you know how you are about remembering things." He says, "Don't have to; I have this nice clear picture in my mind of a hot fudge sundae with pecans on top." So she shrugs her shoulders philosophically, and he leaves. Twenty minutes later he returns and hands her a dozen eggs. She says, "I told you to 'write it down'…you forgot the bacon."

THE DIFFERENCE BETWEEN HEAVEN AND HELL

12.

A preacher is asked by a parishioner, "Tell me, Dr., what is the difference between heaven and hell, exactly?" The ecclesiast replies, "Well let me try to put it in terms that you will readily understand. In heaven the French are the cooks; the Italians are the lovers; the English are the police; the Swiss are the administrators, and the Germans are the mechanics. Whereas, in hell, the English are the cooks; the Swiss are the lovers; the Italians are the mechanics; the French are the administrators, and the Germans are the police."

THE THREE SURGEONS

13.

Three surgeons are having a drink after a round of golf and are discussing what type of patient they prefer to operate on. The first says, "CPA's, because when you open them up you know that what is on the left side is balanced by what is on the right side." The second says, "Engineers, because when you open them up you find that everything is color-coded; if you take out a piece of green tubing, you replace it with another of the same color." The third says; "Attorneys; they're the simplest; there's nothing to worry about; you operate on them, and all there is a mouth and an ass hole, and they're interchangeable!"

CROSS BETWEEN

14.

Question: What do you get when you cross a pit bull with a hooker?
Answer: Your last blow job.

THE INHERITORS

15.

Two black brothers have just been advised that they each have inherited a substantial sum of money from a deceased relative. One asks the other what he plans to do with his inheritance, and he replies, Fust ah'm getting' me a nahs sof' whaht felt hat, and whaht linen suit, a pair of whaht shoes, then a whaht Cadillac convutbl with whaht leathuh seats; then ah'm getting' me a nice lookin' whaht girl; then ah'm gonna drive down to dat small town in Alabama wheah ah growed up and show dem Su'thu'n niggahs how to live. What you gonna do?"

"Well, ah'm getting' me a nahs black felt hat, a black suit, black shoes, a black Caddy convutbl with black leathuh seats; then ah'm findin' me a nahs lookin' black lady; then ah'm gonna follow you down to dat town wheah you growed up and watch dem hang yo' black ass!"

THE SURE BET

16.

The president of DuPont phones the CEO of the Scott Paper Co. and says, "Harry, I have here an invention that my people just developed, which, if I put it on the market, would force your company into bankruptcy, but I'm a friend of yours, so I'm not going to market it."

The other says, "Put my company out of business; that's impossible; the habit of human beings on which we capitalize in the manufacture of Scott Tissue is here to stay; I can conceive of no invention that could do as you claim."

The Pres. of DuPont says, "O.K; since you are so skeptical, I'm going to bet you $10,000.00 that I'm right, and I'll let you be the sole judge of who wins the bet; are you on?" "I'm on," is the reply. "O.K., I'm sending a courier over with a single pill that I want you to take before retiring this evening. Tomorrow morning I want you to call and tell me who wins the bet."

The next day about ten A.M. the CEO of Scott Paper calls his betting pal and says, "You win the bet; I'm sending you over a check for the stipulated amount, and I trust you will donate it to your favorite charity. I took the pill as you said and went to bed. This morning I arose and went into the bathroom and had my regular movement, and it was a substantial one. As I sat there I figured that I had won the bet and reached for our product as usual. It was then that I capitulated; I discovered that I didn't need it at all. I looked in the bowl and there reposed one of the finest, healthiest turds I have ever seen completely wrapped in cellophane!"

AN INTERNATIONAL INQUIRY

17.

One day at the UN a question came up, namely, viz. and to wit: **WHY IS THE HOO-HOO SHAPED THE WAY IT IS?** Since this question has many aspects and was one of global significance several countries undertook to find the definitive answer to the question in question, so to speak.

After spending one hundred million rubles the Russians reported that they had found the answer: It's shape was admirably adapted to facilitating the use of the tube-like configuration for urinating in a wide variety of places and situations thus giving men a slight advantage in this category of human behavior over women, who had been given many advantages over men in other respects.

The French, after spending seven years and 400,000,000 Francs concluded in their report that it was part aesthetic and part utilitarian; the shaft was round to fit snugly into the receptacle that was the vagina in the opposite sex, and the head was so shaped as to facilitate the entrance of the appendage in question into the velvet sheath of love in consummating the act of sexual intercourse.

The Poles, after spending the Polish equivalent of $3.75, and three days, reported that the the head of the hoo-hoo was larger than the shaft so that your hand wouldn't slip off and hit you in the forehead.

THE MIDGET NUN

18.

Picture, if you will...a convent; it is 3:00 AM, and the Mother Superior is awakened by a loud and persistent pounding on the massive front door. She goes to the door, opens the viewing panel and looks out; she sees no one and closes the panel. The pounding immediately resumes, more insistent than ever; she opens the door and peeks out to find two obviously tipsy midgets. She says, "What on earth do you mean about disturbing our convent at this hour of the morning?" One of the midgets says, "Pardon us, Mother Superior, but could you tell us whether there are any midget nuns in your convent?" "She replies, "No, there are not." So he asks, "Well, are there any midget nuns in the county?" "No," she says, "there are none; in fact there are none in the entire state; if there were I would know about it." So the midget who was interrogating the Mother Superior turns to the other and says, "See, I told you that you f ked a penguin."

THE SHORT CUT

19.

Picture, if you will...two youngish nuns returning to the convent after some minimal shopping in a nearby town. It is early evening and getting darkish. They take a shortcut through the woods and are surprised by two men who throw them to the ground and proceed to ravish their bodies. One of the nuns, a white girl, lifts her voice to the heavens and says. "Forgive them, Father, for they know not what they do!" To this the other nun, a black girl, says. "Mine do!"

COHEN AT THE FONTAINEBLEAU

20.

Picture, if you will...Mr. Cohen. a Jewish gentleman from NYC checking into the Fontainebleau Hotel on Miami Beach. He immediately collars an Asst. Mgr. and pulls out a huge roll of bills of impressive denominations and peels off a hundred dollar bill which he gives to the Asst. Mgr. and says, "My name is Cohen, C-O-H-E-N; I'm from New Yawk City, end I vant that you should remembah my face." "Yes, Sir, Mr. Cohen, I'll never forget your face," comes the reply.

Peeling off another hundred dollar bill which he slips to the Asst. Mgr., he says, "I Understand that the Presidential Penthouse suite is occupied; I'd like to move in dere if possible." With this, the Asst Mgr. gets the owner of the hotel on the phone and acquaints him with the situatIon. The owner, Mr. Novak, says,

"Get those people out of that Suite and put Mr. Cohen in… he's one of the really big spenders."

When told that he can move in Mr. Cohen gives the Asst. Mgr. another hundred dollar bill and says, "Now I'm goink up and freshen up a bit; in about a half hour I'll be callink you mit a special order and I vant you should handle it pusnally." "Yes, sir, Mr. Cohen" says the other "I'll await your call."

About a half hour later a call comes through from Mr. Cohen's suite for the Asst. Mgr. "Hello, dis is Mr. Cohen in the Presldentail Penthouse Suite; you remembah me?" "Yes, sir. Mr. Cohen, may I have your order; I'll handle it personally." "Fine," says Cohen, "By fife o'clock dis eftahnoon I vant you should haf delivud to my suite the following items: three negro voigins, they should be fourteen years of age and undah and good lookink; I vant a bull whip, mit knots on the end; I vant two male wrasslers, a minimum of two hundred-fifty pounds each, and a six hundred pound male gorilla; I undastand dat da Ringling Bros. circus has such an animal." "Yes, sir, Mr. Cohen, I'll get right on it."

At four-thirty that afternoon, the Asst Mgr. calls Cohen and says, "About your order, Mr Cohen; I've got the three Negro virgins. two are fourteen, and one is thirteen, and they are all good-looking; I have the bull whip with the knots on the end; I have the two wrestlers who weigh close to three hundred pounds apiece. Now, as to the six hundred pound male gorilla, we have a slight problem; we can't get him here before six-thirty this evening."

Comes back Cohen, "Six-thutty? I said fife o'clock. Cancel the whole order and send up a prune Danish instead."

THE POLISH MAGICIAN

21.

Picture, if you will…the Warsaw Opera House. The Great Wolensky, the renowned Polish magician, is performing. He's down to the last trick of his act, and he calls for a volunteer from the audience to assist him. A young man steps forward and onto the stage. Wolensky whispers to him, "Now ven I geef de signul; you peek op dis beeg vooden mallet and heet me on de hed!" "I cannot do dees," says the young man, "dis vood keel you!" Wolensky says, "Trost me, I'm a magician; eet's a treek, okay?"

So the volunteer on signal from Wolensky, picks up the mallet and hits him on the head. The magician crumples to the stage and is rushed to the hospital where he remains in a coma day after day, week after week, month after month. Well, the young man who had wielded the mallet feels so guilty that he sits by his bedside constantly.

Then, about six months after the incident, the young man notices that Wolensky's eyelids are fluttering, and suddenly his eyes pop open. He sees the young, man sitting there, and, raising his right hand high, he says, "**TA-DAAAAAAH!**"

THE PREPOSITIONS

22.

Picture, if you will, a young lad sick in bed at home. His aunt drops by to see him and on the way upstairs to his room selects a book from the library to read to him. She enters the sick room, sits down on the edge of the bed and opens the book. The lad takes one look at the book and says, "Oh, Aunty, what did you bring that book I didn't want to get read to out of up for?"

THE FIVE ANDS

23.

This is a conundrum of sorts to test your knowledge of grammar and usage of the English language. The question is: Can you make up a sentence that contains five "and's" in a row that makes sense and is grammatically acceptable? Give up? Okay, here it is: Harry Smith and Fred Jones decide to open a hardware store, so they engage the services of a sign painter to do a sign to be mounted over the front door saying, "Smith and Jones, Hardware."

The painter works all day, and finally he is finished at about five p.m. and asks Messrs. Smith and Jones to step outside to see the new sign. Well, upon inspection, they notice that the sign painter has run their names together so that the sign reads, "SMITHANDJONES HARDWARE". This, of course is unsatisfactory, and Smith says, "no! no! no! That's not what we want; there should be a space between 'Smith' and 'and' and 'and' and 'Jones!'"

VISITING DAD AT THE HOME

24.

Picture, if you will...an Old Folks' Home. A young man is visiting his father, who is in a wheelchair; they are out on the porch where such visits customarily take place. During the course of their conversation the old gentleman starts to lean to the right very slowly. This is promptly noticed by an attendant who props him up and stuffs a small pillow down between him and the side of the wheelchair. The conversation proceeds, and the old gentleman starts leaning to the right very slowly. Ever alert, the attendant again props him upright and stuffs another small pillow between him and the other side of the wheelchair. Again they resume the conversation, and the old gentleman starts to lean forward very slowly. Again the attendant props him up and adjusts the two small pillows so that he is upright again. At this point the son says to his father, "Say, Dad, how do you like it here at the home?" His dad replies, "It's okay, but they won't let me fart!"

THE ESKIMO MOTORIST

25.

Picture, if you will…an Eskimo woman driving along the highway in Alaska. She looks in her rear-view mirror and notices that her car is emitting great clouds of smoke, so she stops at the next service station and tells the mechanic what she has observed. He pops the hood, looks around inside and then turns to the woman and says, "Looks like you blew a seal." With this, the woman wipes something off the side of her mouth and says, "No, that's just some mayonnaise from my sandwich!"

THE SCIENTIFIC BREAKTHROUGH

26.

Picture, if you will…a scientific meeting. An eminent research biologist is there to address a group of his colleagues who are there to hear what he has to say about a rumored breakthrough he has made. He is on the dais, and the hall is full. He says, "I am pleased to announce a significant breakthrough! We have managed to create human life in the laboratory; in the test tube, so to speak!" Everyone leans forward expectantly. This is indeed a significant breakthrough.

The speaker continues, "I shall now tell you how we did this. Here in my left hand we have in this vial Solution A, a synthesized amalgam of the chemical constituents of the male spermatozoon. And over here in my right hand in this vial we have Solution B, a valid infusion of the component elements of the female ovum. Now, if we mix Solution A and Solution B in a third vial with a catalytic agent under laboratory conditions of standard temperature and pressure, we get human life!"

With this, the crowd goes wild, everyone is talking at once. This is what science has been attempting to accomplish since time immemorial. Finally he gets the audience to quiet down and says, "Are there any questions?" A man in the back says, "Yes, Doctor; would you mind giving us a demonstration?" "I'd like to," says the speaker, "but it seems that Solution B has a headache!!"

THE NEIMAN MARCUS STORY

27.

Project yourselves back into the past to the time when there was only one Neiman-Marcus Store, in Dallas, TX. Now, picture, if you will…a young couple shopping there. He has to go to the men's room, so he beckons to a floor walker. The floor walker approaches; he is very suavely attired: striped trousers, swallow-tail coat, cravat, stick pin, and boutonniere. He says, "May I help you, sir?" "Yes, you can; where's the men's room please?"

"Well," says the floor walker, "just proceed through this ivory and gold arch on the left and ascend to the second level; wend your way through the Italian Gallery of Renaissance Art, thence through the Peacock Court of Persian Rugs,

Draperies and Antiques, and just beyond you will find the accommodations you seek."

So he takes off as instructed, and twenty minutes later he returns. His wife is standing there tapping her foot impatiently and says, "Just where have you been, and what took you so long?" "Well," says her husband, "I went through this ivory and gold arch on the left and ascended to the second level; I wended my way through the Italian Gallery of Renaissance Art, thence through the Peacock Court of Persian Rugs, Draperies and Antiques and into the exquisite and luxurious accommodations of the Gentlemen's Lounge. Well, when I took it out, it looked so shabby, wrinkled and unimpressive, I took it down the street to the Texaco Station!"

THE DENTIST SHOP

28.

Picture, if you will...a dentist's office. A man comes running in, right through the waiting room where there are several people who have appointments, right past the receptionist's station and into the dentist's room. He plops himself down in the chair, unzips his fly and pulls out his hoo-hoo. The dentist comes flying in and says, "What are you doing there? You don't even have an appointment; there are people waiting out there who do have appointments. Furthermore, you're sitting there holding your exposed member. I'm a dentist; I'm sure you must know that I deal in teeth." "Yes," he says, "that's why I'm here, there's a tooth in it!"

THE POST OFFICE IS HIRING

29.

Picture, if you will...a young man being interviewed for a job with the U.S Postal System. He has answered an ad that says that Veterans would be given preference. The interviewer says, "Your application says that you were injured in Vietnam." "Yes, I was; my testicles were shot off." The interviewer says, "This interview is over; you've got the job. We open at nine tomorrow, you come in at ten, and we'll put you right to work." "Excuse me," says the young man, "if you open at nine, why do you want me to come in at ten?" The man replies, "Well, in the post office for the first hour we just stand around scratching our balls!"

RODEO STYLE

30.

A man says to his friend, "Have you and your wife ever done it Rodeo style?" The friend says, "Rodeo style; what's that?" The man replies, "Well, your wife lies face down on the bed, you mount her from behind and whisper in her ear, 'This is how my secretary and I do it,' and then try to hang on for eight seconds!!"

FOR THE SINS OF YOUR LIFE

31.

Picture, if you will…the reception room in Heaven; sitting together are three men: Teddy Kennedy, William Jefferson Clinton and (here insert the name of a friend).

Over the loud speaker comes a message, "Teddy Kennedy, please report to the Blue Room;" the message is repeated, so the three proceed to the Blue Room to see what awaits Teddy Kennedy. Teddy opens the door to a what is a very sparsely furnished bed room. There sitting on the bed is an 87-year-old hag, stark naked, her scrawny body wrinkled and unlovely; her toothless mouth is revealed as she says, "Come in, Teddy Kennedy; you are now mine for all eternity." And from the intercom they hear, "For the sins you committed while on Earth, Teddy Kennedy, this is your reward." Clinton and (name of friend) are pretty shook up, wondering what's in store for them. They return to the reception room.

Next, the message comes across on the loud speaker, "William Jefferson Clinton, please report to the Red room; Clinton to the Red Room." So he and (name of friend) proceed to the Red room to see what fate awaits Bill Clinton. The latter opens the door to the designated chamber, and in the wretchedly furnished bed room is a big, fat, ugly, filthy, naked, sweating and obviously homosexual black person who says, "Come in Slick Willie, you are now mine for all eternity!" And over the intercom comes, "William Jefferson Clinton, for the sins you committed while on Earth, this is your reward!" The one remaining member of the original trio returns to the reception room visibly shaken.

Then the loud speaker says, "(name of friend) please report to the Gold Room." So he complies and opens the door to the quarters thus indicated. He is dumbfounded. He's in the most beautiful and luxuriously furnished bed room he has ever seen, an exact copy of the Honeymoon Suite at the Waldorf-Astoria. There, sitting on the huge round bed, clad only in the latest negligee from Victoria's Secret is Sharon Stone, her beautiful blonde tresses glistening upon her shoulders. She says, "Come in (name of friend), you are now mine for all eternity." And from the intercom system, "For the sins you committed while upon Earth, Sharon Stone, this is your reward!"

THE ELDERLY BROTHEL CUSTOMER

32.

Picture, if you will…a house of ill repute. An 85-year-old gentleman comes in and makes his halting way over to the desk where the madam transacts her business. She observes his progress, shrugs her shoulders philosophically, and says, "What can we do for you today, Sir?" To which he replies, "I'd like a young, maybe twenty or twenty-one year old blonde girl, slender, nice boobs; took my Viagra just an hour ago." The madam says, "Well go on up to room 2b, Emily will take good care of you; she fits your description."

He proceeds to Room 2b and there is Emily who certainly does conform to his expressed preferences. She removes her wrapper and lies down on the bed to await developments; she is ready.

The old gentleman then takes off his coat and hangs in neatly on the back of a chair. Then, in turn, he removes the rest of his clothes and also places them neatly on the chair. Having stripped to the buff, he reaches into a pocket of the coat, removes a condom and proceeds to put it on. Emily, says, "You don't need that; we girls in this establishment are clean and sanitary." He says, "I don't like to take chances!" So Emily shrugs her shoulders philosophically.

He then reaches into another pocket and brings out a large ball of cotton. He pulls pieces of cotton off the ball and stuffs them up both of his nostrils and into each ear. "What on earth are you doing?" says Emily. In reply to which the old gentleman says, "There are two things I can't stand: a screamin' woman and the smell of burnin' rubber!!"

THE DIAGNOSIS

33.

Picture, if you will…a black doctor's office located in an area wherein black residents predominate. He has just that day hung out his shingle and is waiting for his first patient. He has placed in his right hand desk drawer a five by seven inch card printed in large letters which he had received from the ancient doctor who was his mentor. It contained three rules:

1. ALWAYS GET YOUR CONSULTATION FEE IN ADVANCE.
2. ALWAYS MAKE A PROMPT DIAGNOSIS.
3. NEVER GO BACK ON YOUR DIAGNOSIS.

The first patient arrives, and before he has a chance to initiate a recitation of his ills, the doctor checks the card and says, "Befo' we gets goin' heah, ah needs a consultation fee of fi' dollahs." The patient come up with the stipulated amount, and the doctors says, "Now, tell me brothah, whu's de trouble you done got?" To which the man says, "Doctuh, ah got de wust cramps in mah stummick dat ah's evah suffud!" The doctor consults his card again and says, "Ah knose whut de problem is heah; you done got a locked bowel." The man says, "It cain't be dat, doctuh; cus accompanyin' de cramps ah's done got a bad case of diarrhea." The doctor checks his card again and says without hesitation, "Yes, you done got you a locked bowel au raht, an' its locked in the open position!!"

AUNTY'S REMAINS

34.

It seems that a very wealthy English lady died while on a trip up the Nile, so her nephew, and sole heir, takes it upon himself to see to it that her remains are returned to London for a proper burial. When the casket arrives in due course at the funeral establishment theretofore designated by her nephew, Reginald Smythe-Featherstone, he decides to take one last look at his benefactress, so he has the casket opened and is shocked to find that his aunt's remains are not there in the casket as expected; rather he finds the remains of a Russian general in his dress uniform.

So he immediately cables the British Ambassador in Moscow to alert him to the mistake and suggests that action be taken promptly before it's too late.

Two days later he receives a cablegram from Moscow from the British Ambassador which reads, "Do what you wish with the remains of the Russian General; your aunt has been buried with full military honors!"

FATHER, SON AND CAR

35.

Picture, if you will…a father conversing with his teenage son who is a junior in high school. The boy tells his father that he needs a car to keep up with his peers. The father says, "I'll make a deal with you; if by the next report your grade average is at least a B, and if you read the Bible every day and get that long hair cut off, I'll get you a car. Okay?"

The next report comes out and the boy has four B's and an A; his father tells him that he is proud of him for making such a fine effort in school. Then he finds that the boy has been reading the Bible daily, but notes that he has not had the long hair shorn.

The father declares that the conditions have not yet been met, and the son says, "Well, I read in the Bible that Jesus never cut his hair, and you have always told me that he is a good role model." "That's fine," his father says, "but you should have read further, for in the Bible it is said, '…and Jesus walked wherever he went.'"

BIG DEAL IN FRANKFURT

36.

An American businessman is in Frankfurt, West Germany, to conclude a multi-million dollar deal; this will take about five days to finalize. His host is a billionaire German industrialist who, as a friendly gesture, arranges for him to have the intimate services of an elegant call girl for the duration of his stay.

On the fiftth day, the deal having been successfully put to bed, the American businessman is about to leave his hotel for the airport. He takes out his wallet and extracts five one-hundred-dollar bills which he hands to the girl as a gratuity. She says, "Vass is diss?" He replies, "This is five hundred dollars United States currency." She says, "Marks; I vant marks!!" "Okay", he says, "A+ on the sucking; B+ on the f king, and C- on the foreplay!"

FIRST MAN, FIRST WOMAN, FIRSTS PROBLEM

37.

Picture, if you will…the Garden of Eden. Adam wakes up; he doesn't know what he is or where he is. A voice comes down from the heavens; the voice says, "This is God speaking; you are Adam, the first man on Earth; I am going to pluck from your side a rib and from that rib I am going to create a woman; her name will be Eve. You will mate with Eve and you will have children; your children will have children and they will have children and their children will have children, *ad infinitum*, and you will thereby populate the Earth. After giving Adam some further details and instruction, God does indeed do the rib plucking bit and creates Eve, and she is beautiful. After Eve has been brought up to speed on what has eventuated and what the future will bring, God says, "Now you will need a place where you two can mate, and I have provided such a place for you. Behind that bush on your left, in the side of the hill there is a very comfortable cave where you can do this, and remember, if you have any questions, I am always near."

So Adam and Eve retire to the cave for mating purposes. After about ten minutes Adam appears outside the cave, and lifting his face to the heavens, he says, "God, are you there?" "Yes, my son, I am here; do you have a question?" "Yes," says Adam, **"WHAT'S A HEADACHE?"**

HORSE MANEUVERS

38.

Picture, if you will…two men and a horse. One says to the other, "I'll bet you a hundred bucks that I can make your horse laugh." The owner takes the bet, and the other sidles up to the horse and whispers something in his ear. The horse breaks out in raucous laughter, so his owner pays up.

The winner then proposes a new bet: for a hundred, he bets he can make the horse cry. The owner accepts the bet confident that he will win his money back. Thereupon, the other takes the horse behind the barn, and two minutes later he brings the horse back, and the horse is indeed weeping copiously.

Again the owner pays up, but then asks if the other will reveal how he made the horse laugh and then cry. "It was easy," he says, "first I whispered in his ear that my hoo-hoo is bigger than his, and he laughed. Then when I took him behind the barn I showed it to him!"

ROUGH DAY IN UBANGILAND

39.

Picture, if you will…the family mud hit in Ubangiland; it is evening, and the husband has just come home from his hunting. He looks around and says, "Iki oglu wassa naka zum bogu noga loka bondu!" which means, "Here I come home from a long hard day hunting the great white elephant, and what do I find? The dishes are piled up in the sink; there's dust all over and the garbage hasn't been taken out!"

His wife explains, "Naga ugu laka bugu zum natta rika baga naka zum!" which means, "I'm sorry Darling it's such a mess, but the schvartze didn't show up today!"

A LADY OF CULTURE

40.

Picture, if you will…the annual election meeting of the Southern Abyssinian Baptist Church in a small town of Alabama. The preacher is speaking. "Now y'all has de slate fum de nominatin' committee; iz dey any mo' nominations fum de flo'?"

A hand shoots up; it's a lady in the back of the hall. After being recognized by the preacher who is the chairperson for this meeting, she says, "Rev'run, ah wishes to put in nomination fo de office of president de name of mahsef. As y'all knose, las' yeah ah wuz defeated fo dat office 'cause y'all din't think ah had no culchuh. Well, to bring y'all up to date on dat subject of whethah ah duz have culchuh, lemme review mah activities of dis past yeah. Now who wuz it dat visited de Rev'run in de hospital evra day fo' two weeks he was deah an' dat arranged de flowahs so purty? It is ah, das who, an y'all say I doan have no culchuh. An' who wuz it dat done conducted de choir rehearsals evra Thu'sday naht de whole yeah? It iz ah, das who dun all dat. An' y'all say I doan have no culchuh. An' who's bin de spahk plug fo' the wimmin's guild dat dun decorated de altuh evra Sunday? It is ah, an' y'all say I doan have no culchuh…sheeee-it!"

THE BIRD WITH THE BROKEN WING

41.

Picture, if you will…a sparrow in a hailstorm. He is struck by a large hailstone which fractures his wing. He spins in and happens to land in a pasture. He is cold, miserable and unhappy, and his wing hurts. Shortly after realizing the full extent of his plight, along comes a cow and dumps a load right on top of him. The bird is chagrined and humiliated but has to admit that what has dropped upon him is warm, moist and soothing to his damaged wing. However, the ignominy of the situation wins out and he pokes his head out from the pile and starts to scream, holler and chirp at the top of his lungs to voice his frustration. A wolf happens to hear all the commotion and investigates. Seeing the bird in its helpless condition, he digs him out and gobbles him up.

This story has three morals:

1. Someone who shits on you is not necessarily an enemy.
2. Someone who digs you out of a pile of shit is not necessarily a friend.

3. If you are cozy, snug and warm in a pile of shit, keep your head down and your mouth shut!

RELATIVE HUMIDITY

42.

Relative humidity is defined as the sweat that forms on your balls when you get caught screwing your cousin.

UNCLE CHARLEY'S PECCADILLO

43.

Picture, if you will...a very elegant house of ill repute on Park Lane in London. A young English chap of obvious good breeding is entering the premises and is surprised and disturbed to see his Uncle Charley, a member of the House of Lords, descending the stairs. He says, "Uncle Charley! I'm shocked to see you in a place like this, a man of your position!"

"Well, my boy," says Uncle Charley, "it's like this: where sex is concerned I much prefer the vigor and enthusiasm of the young ladies of this establishment to the dignified acquiescence of your dear Aunt Maude!"

POOR DOOLEY

44.

Picture, if you will...two Irishmen meeting on the street; one is named Pat and the other, Mike. Pat says, "Mike, did ya hear wot hoppened to poor Dooley?" "No," says Mike, "wot hoppened to poor Dooley?" "Well," says Pat, "it seems that he fell in a barrel of beer, and he drowned, he did!" "Oh, thot's mighty sad, says, Mike, "didn't have a chance, eh." To which Pat replies, "Not exactly. He got out twice to go to the men's room!"

COMPLAINTS

45.

Picture, if you will...a junior executive in a large company; he has just virtually stormed into the office of the CEO right past a vigorously protesting secretary. He's very upset and says. "Frankly, I've just about reached my limit!" "Now, calm down, Frank," says the big boss; if you have complaints, tell me about it, and we'll see if something can be done to correct the situation to your satisfaction!"

"Do I have complaints? You bet I have, and I'll enumerate them: first of all, I don't think I'm being paid what I'm worth, taking into account the responsibilities of my position. Next, the secretary I have not only can't type or take shorthand, but she has both B.O and halitosis. Third, that office to which I was assigned has about as much privacy as Grand Central Station; I'm practically in the hall. And, lastly, about half the personnel around her seem to be gay!"

"All right, let's see what we can do for you here; first, your salary; you'll find a 50% raise reflected in your next pay check, and we'll make the raise retroactive for six months. Next, fire your secretary and hire another one to suit you, salary, no object, your discretion. Next, your office; one of our vice presidents in moving to St. Louis; you can move into his suite, spacious, nice view, and you can redecorate any way you want, and the company will pick up the tab. There, does that satisfy you?" "It sure does, in fact it's quite generous; thanks a lot!" says the jr. exec. "Fine," says the CEO, "now kiss me and get back to work!"

MOTHER THERESA?

46.

Picture, if you will…two guys walking along the sidewalk on the West side of Park Avenue, Central Park East. One says, "Hey, Jack, look at that old lady over there; I think that's Mother Theresa." "Yeah," says Jack, "it sure looks like her; let's go see." So, they go over to the lady in question and Jack says, "Excuse us, lady, but are you by chance Mother Theresa?" To this the lady replies, "F k off, you ass holes!!" So they move off, and Jack says, "I guess we'll never know, huh?"

THE GOAT WAGON

47.

Picture, if you will…a man walking down the street; he spies a little boy sitting in a shiny new red wagon to which is attached a goat complete with reins, bridle and of all things, a third rein that is attached to the goat's testicles. He stops and says to the little boy, "Say, that's a fine rig you have there, Sonny."

"Thank you, sir," he replies, "when I pull this rein here, that goat goes to the right, and when I pull the left rein he goes to the left."

"What's that other string there that you have tied to the goat's jewels?, says the man.

"Oh," says the little boy, "that's my passing gear!!"

IN FLAGRANTE DELICTO

48.

Picture, if you will…a small frame house in Coconut Grove, a trendy suburb of Miami. A couple is in bed making love. Everything is progressing smoothly when they hear a car pulling into the carport on the side of the house. "MiGod," says the woman, "that's my husband; he's home a day early. Quick! You've got to get out of here."

"Right," says the man, scooping up his clothes, "where's the back door?"

"We don't have a back door! She says.
He says, "Okay; where do you want one?"

THE BRUSH FIRE

49.

Two Polacks have been hired by a movie company to help control a small brush fire that has been deliberately set in connection with a film sequence in a major motion picture. The super who hired them goes to check on them. because the fire seems to be getting a little out of control.

The two were not on the job, and the man finally spots their pick-up truck over in another area and then spots them on the edge of some woods nearby. One of them has his pants down and is bending over; the other appears to be buggering him.

"What the Hell's going on here; I hired you two guys to watch the fire, and here I find you involved in a disgusting perverted act. What do you have to say for yourselves?"

The active member of the duo says, "Gee, Boss, my buddy inhaled a lot of smoke when the wind shifted, and I tried to help him out…"

"Why you dumb Polack, you're supposed to give mouth-to-mouth resuscitation for that," says the super.

To which the other says, "How do you think this got started?"

FINNEGAN AND FLAHERTY

50.

Finnegan and Flaherty were the best of friends, and every Friday at 5:00 PM they they would meet in the same little pub and drink Irish whiskey, tell Irish jokes and sing Irish songs and get very pleasantly snockered. Well this routine went on for minny minny months, until one Friday when neither showed up at the appointed time. This mildly disturbs the bartender, because he looks forward to these sessions.

Finally, two hours later Flaherty comes in; he's a bloody mess, clothing torn and disheveled, contusions, abrasions and lacerations about the head, limbs and body. He orders a double shot of Jameson's and downs it.

"Wot hoppened to ya, Flaherty?" says the bartender somewhat aghast.

"Finnegan hoppened to me that's wot," says Flaherty, "and at the time he had in his hand a large monkey wrench, he did!"

"Is that right?" says the bartender, "and what did you have in your hand?"

"Mrs. Finnegan's ass," says Flaherty, "and let me tell you something, it's no help in a fight!"

MOSES RETURNS FROM THE MOUNTAIN

51.

Moses is coming down the mountain. He says to the crowd that has gathered at the foot of the mountain, "I know you are all anxious to hear what has been happening up there on the mountain. Well, I have been negotiating with God for the past couple of days as you know, about the Commandments, and I mean he is one tough negotiator, let me tell you! But I think we have a deal (loud cheers). I have good news and I have bad news; the good news is that I have him down to ten; the bad news is: Adultery stays in!!"

NEW WONDER DRUGS

52.

Sexamyacin: It keeps your back from petering out and your peter from backing out.

Mentholated Ex-Lax: For a cool stool.

Spantran: A compound of Spanish Fly and a tranquilizing drug:

Take this and you're always ready for sex, but if you don't get any, you really don't care.

THE BOSS

53.

When the body was first made, all the parts wanted to be "boss". The brain said, "Since I control everything, I should be boss."

The feet said, "Since I carry man wherever he goes and get him into position to do what the brain wants, I should be boss."

The hands said, "Since I do all the work and earn all the money to keep the rest of you going, I should be boss."

And so it went with the heart, the eyes, the ears and the lungs. Finally the ass hole spoke up and demanded that he be made boss. All the other parts laughed uproariously at the idea of the ass hole being boss.

The ass hole was so angered that he blocked himself off and refused to function. Soon the brain was feverish; the eyes crossed and ached, the feet were to weak to walk, and the hands hung limply at the sides; the heart and the lungs struggled to keep going. All the parts pleaded with the brain to relent and let the ass hole be boss. And so it went; all the other parts did all the work, and the ass hole bossed and passed out a lot of shit.

The moral of this story is: You don't have to be a brain to be boss – just an ass hole!

THE DISROBING

54.

Picture, if you will...a fine mansion with a circular driveway edged with meticulously manicured hedges and flower beds and the like. A Rolls limousine turns into the driveway and stops at the front door under the neo-Greek portico. A tall handsome chauffeur steps out, opens the rear door and assists an elegant and beautiful middle-aged lady to alight.

She says to the chauffeur, "Charles, please come into the house for a minute." He opens the door for her and follows her in.

She says, "Charles, let's go into the library," and they do. She then says, "Please close the door," which he does.

At this point she looks him right in the eyes and says: "Charles unzip my dress and take it off (he does); now unfasten my bra and take that off (he complies); all right, now my slip (he takes that off); finally, take off my panty hose (he does this). Now Charles, she continues, I want to make sure that you understand; if I ever catch you wearing my clothes again, you're fired!!"

THE SUPER SALESMAN

55.

Picture, if you will...a suite of offices – big company – very plush. A salesman comes in and speaks to the secretary of the president, object: to see the president. She advises him that the president has not yet arrived, that he is a very busy man and that when he does arrive, he won't see him. The salesman says, "Oh yes, he will, and what's more I'll sell him a big order!"

The president arrives, and the salesman talks him into seeing him. "I'll give you five minutes," he says.

Five minutes later the salesman comes out into the secretary's area and shows her the order, and it is big. He then says, "This order means so much to me that I'm, going to take you out to a fine restaurant and we're going to toast this order with champagne!" "Oh no, you're not!" she says.

"Yes, I am, and not only that, but after dinner we're going over to your place for a night cap, and we're going to make love!" "Oh no, were not!" she says. "Oh yes, we are! And not only that, I'm not going to use a condom!" he says. And she says, "Oh yes, you are!!!

SNOW WHITE AND THE SEVEN DWARFS

56.

Snow White assembles the 7 dwarfs one evening and tells them that the Prince has invited her to be his date for the big annual ball at his castle the following Saturday night. She says that she feels obligated to accept since they are living on his land rent free. The seven are terribly jealous and grumble a lot, but they have to admit the validity of the premise.

Well, Saturday evening arrives, and the seven dwarfs decide to spy on the Prince and Snow White about whom they feel very protective. They peek in through the window while the dancing is in progress, and when that part of the evening is over and the guests have left, they see the Prince pick up Snow White in his arms and stride up the long winding staircase.

They step back and look upward and see a light come on in what they assume is his bedroom. Now they are really concerned, and they wonder how they can see what is going on up there and conclude that the only way they can spy on the Prince and Snow White is to stand on each other's shoulders, stacked up, if you will, so that the top dwarf, the smallest one, is just barley able to see over the window sill and into the Prince's bedroom. It is his job to relay down the stack of dwarfs what he is observing so that they will all be advised.

The top dwarf, says, "The Prince is kissing Snow White," and so it goes down the stack, "The Prince is kissing Snow White, "The Prince is kissing Snow White," and so on.

"He's carrying her to the bed." "He's carrying her to the bed." "He's carrying her to the bed." Etc. etc.

"He's undressing her." He's Undressing her. He's Undressing her." etc. etc.

"He's kissing her breasts." He's kissing her breasts." "He's kissing her breasts." etc. etc.

Just then the Prince happens to glance over at the window and he spies the nose and hands of the top dwarf on the window sill, so gets up and advances toward the window to see what's going on. This alarms the one who is peeking over the window sill, and he says to the dwarf directly below him, "The Prince is coming!" Then on down the stack:

> "Me, too!"
> "Me, too!"
> "Me, too!"
> "Me, too!"
> "Me, too!"
> "Me, too!"

A GOOD AMERICAN STEAK

57.

A couple from Texas traveling in England for two weeks have just returned to London. The husband says, "Boy, am I ever tired of this English food, mutton chops, sweetbreads, Shepherd's Pie, and all. What I want is a good American steak cooked properly. Let's finesse London and hop right over to Paris (their next stop) I know I can get a good steak at the Ritz!"

The wife replies, "We can't just hop over to Paris at this juncture; we have too many obligations here in London; there are too many people we still have to see, but don't worry about your good American steak; I hear that the Dorchester Hotel features such a steak."

So he says, "Okay, I'll make a deal with you: if the Dorchester has a good American steak, I'll get off your back."

So they go to the Dorchester that evening, and he is pleased to see on the menu with a red border, "A Good American Steak for our friends from the United States, cooked to order." "Ah, we're back in civilization!" he says.

He gets ahold of a waiter, gives him a fiver and says, "I want one of these steaks, cooked medium rare, okay? Now write it down so there won't be any question about it." The waiter does as he's told, "Yes, sah, steak, medium rare, I've got it."

Well, when the steak arrives, it's cooked well done, and this irritates him greatly, so he tells the waiter, "Tell the chef to try again; I can't eat this. I want it medium rare; I saw you write that down."

The waiter then in due course brings a steak that is warm on both sides, too rare for the man, so he says, "Well, we're getting somewhere, anyway; now take this back to the chef and tell him to do it two more minutes on each side, and then it should be fine." So the waiter writes down "Two minutes, each side, yes sah!"

Well, the waiter brings it back again, and it is cooked to pieces. The man is justifiably irate and tells the waiter, "Now, son, I have special instructions for the chef: take this steak back and tell him to shove it up his ass! Have you got that?" "Yes, sah, 'up his ass'; I've got that."

About three minutes pass and the waiter reappears and says, "Dreadfully sorry, sah, but there will be a slight delay; there are two lamb chops in front of us!!"

THE DIET

58.

Picture, if you will…a doctor's office. A young man is being interviewed by the doctor to whom he has been referred by his primary physician. He weighs slightly over 300 lbs and has been told that unless is loses 120 lbs. or so, his life will be greatly foreshortened.

The doctor tells him, "Now my diet is somewhat unusual; you can eat all you want of anything you want; the only thing is that you have to take all your food anally, not orally." The patient is ready to try anything; he is scared.

About six months later the doctor and the patient bump into each other on the street. The Doctor says, "You look familiar, but I can't seem to place you." The other says, "I'm one of your patients that has been on that anal diet of yours. I'm down to 180; the last time you saw me I was over 300!"

At this point the doctor notices that his patient is almost frantically shifting from foot to foot, and he says, "Yes, I do remember you, and that weight loss is fantastic; you look very good, but that strange side-effect you have there, moving about nervously; we'll we have to see what we can do about that."

"Not to worry, Doc," he replies, "I'm just chewing gum!!"

<u>GAY AND FRIVOLOUS</u>

a.

59.

Picture, if you will…an army induction station. The recruits are there to take their physicals following which they are scheduled to be interviewed by a psychiatrist who is seated at a table off to the side.

The doctor is signing a paper pertaining to the last man he interviewed and looks up and sees an obviously gay fellow sort of swishing like some of them do. The doctor shrugs his shoulders philosophically and looks the fellow in the eye and says, "Do you actually think you could kill a man?"

"Well, yes, but it might take me three or four days!!"

b.

Picture, if you will a deli. A gay fellow is looking around the store, and after about five minutes the proprietor comes over to him and says, "Is there something I can do for you, young man?" "Yes, there is," he replies, "I think I'd like that salami hanging over there." "Would you like me to slice it for you?" asks the proprietor. To which the other replies, "Of course not; what do you think I am, a piggy bank?"

c.

Picture, if you will a proctologist's office. A young gay is there to see the doctor. It seems that he has developed a fearful crush on the doctor, and he makes all kinds of excuses to come in to see him. This sort of irritates the doctor, because he has no similar personal feeling for the fellow. He says, "Well, what is it today?" sort of curtly. The gay says, "Look in my ass." So the doctor says, "Drop your pants, turn around, bend over and spread your cheeks." The gay complies, and the doctor notices something protruding from his anus and upon removing it he has in his hand a long-stem red rose. And he sees another and another, and finally he has withdrawn a dozen roses from his ass. He says, "You boob! What are you doing with a dozen long-stem roses up your ass?" The gay says, "**Read the card!!!**"

d.

A gay visits his proctologist. The doctor says, "What is it that I can do for you today, young man?" To which he replies, "Oh Doctor, I have a vibrator stuck up my ass, and I need help." "Don't worry, son, we'll have that out of there in jig time." "No, no," says the gay, "just replace the batteries."

GOOD ADVICE FROM A WISE OLD MAN

60.

When promulgating your esoteric cogitations or articulating your philosophical or metaphysical meanderings, beware of platitudinous ponderosity. Let you extemporaneous expatiations and unpremeditated decantings have intelligibility and veracity without thrasonical bombast. Seduously avoid all polysyllabic profundity, psittaceous vacuity, vaniloquent vapidity and pestiferous profanity. Speak briefly, clearly, concisely, candidly and purely; say what you mean, mean what you say, and above all, **DON'T USE BIG WORDS!!!**

SISTER HORTENSIA

61.

At the end of World War II in Italy an Army Lieutenant was given the duty to inform the Mother Superior of the Sacred Heart Convent that the war was over so she and her sisters could relax. This convent was high in the mountains and very difficult to access, so the Lt. Checked out a jeep, and took his Sgt. as a driver to make the trip.

They made it all right, and the Lt. was promptly ushered into the Mother Superior's reception room. He said, "We are pleased to be able to tell you, Mother Superior, that as far as Italy is concerned, the war is over. Tell me what it was like for you and the sisters while the war was in progress?"

She said, "Well, it was terrible; first we were overrun by drunken Italian soldiers who raped us all, all except for Sister Hortensia, of course. Then the Germans stormed through the convent and raped us all, except for Sister Hortensia, of course. After that, a unit of Yugoslavs that were attached to Axis Forces invaded our sanctuary and raped all of us, except for Sister Hortensia, of course."

At this point the Lt. interrupted the recitation and said, "You say that these three groups of soldiers got out of control and raped all of you up here except for Sister Hortensia? How come Sister Hortensia never got raped?"

"Oh! Sister Hortensia didn't like that sort of thing!"

THE BIG CHIEF AND THE BROTHEL

62.

Picture, if you will…a small town in New Mexico. The venue is the local brothel; an impressive-looking Indian Chief has just entered. He has just cashed his monthly gov't. check. The Madam says, "How, Chief; what chief want?" He replies, "Chief want woman; young, slender, blonde, nice boobs!"

The Madam says, "Does Chief have money?" "Yes, Chief has money" With this he pulls out his roll. "Does Chief have experience?" "No, Chief doesn't have experience." "Well, Chief," she says, "I can't let you in if you don't have experience; it would be unfair to my girls and embarrassing for you."

"Where Chief get experience?" he asks. "Okay Chief I'll tell you what to do. Go down to the end of this street and on the left you will see a store called 'Al's Grocery'; you go in there and give Al two dollars, and he will see to it that you get experience; tell him I sent you."

So the Chief does as instructed and after paying Al the stipulated sum, Al takes him out behind the store where there are a lot of stumps and big trees with knotholes of various sizes and heights off the ground. Al says, "Just pick one your size and height, stick your hoo-hoo into it and hump, hump, hump, like that. This will give you experience."

The next scene is one month later; again the Chief has just cashed his check and made his way to the brothel in question. After he has advised the Madam that he now has both cash and experience, she says, "You go upstairs to Room 2, and Emily will take good care of you."

So he does that, and there is Emily and she conforms to his expressed wishes concerning her physical appearance. He says, "Take off clothes." And she complies. "All right, now bend over and grab ankles." This is not an unusual request in her line of work, so she does as told.

With Emily in that position, Chief takes out from under his blanket a big stick and whacks Emily smartly on the ass. She grabs her injured ass and cries out, "You cockamamie Indian! What the hell are you doing?" He replies, **"Chief check for bees!!!"**

THE RETIRED ADMIRAL AND THE BROTHEL

63.

Picture, if you will…a nicely appointed brothel in Virginia Beach. A retired 85-year-old Admiral has entered and is speaking with the Madam. She knows the Admiral and is acquainted with his limitations, so she gets the money, picks out the youngest, sexiest young lady on her staff and sends them up to Room 3-B. The girl lies down on the bed, unzips her wrapper, lays it open, and she is ready. The Admiral strips to the buff and mounts her. He is humping and grinding away with apparent enthusiasm and says, "How'm I doin'?" She answers, "You're doing three knots, Admiral." "Three knots, what do you mean?" She replies, "You're not up, you're not in, and you're not getting your money back!!"

BLIND ENCOUNTER

64.

Picture, if you will...a blind bunny rabbit. Because he's blind he doesn't know what he is, so one day he sets off into the woods in search of someone who can tell him what he is. While thus engaged he bumps into a blind snake. The rabbit says, "Please excuse me, but I am blind; I wonder if you would be so kind as to tell me what I am?"

"Well, I'd like to do that for you, but unfortunately I also am blind. I have a suggestion: I'll feel you all over and describe what you look like, and maybe we can give a good guess what you are; and then you can do the same for me."

"That sounds like a good idea," says the bunny. So the other feels around and says, "Well, you have two long floppy ears, a fuzzy round ball of a tail and whiskers. Maybe you are a rabbit." The rabbit says, "Yes, that makes sense, because I love lettuce and thump my hind foot on the ground a lot; I must indeed be a bunny rabbit; thank you so much; now let me do the same for you."

Then the rabbit feels the other all over, and says, "Well, you have very little cranial capacity and no backbone, you're low down and slimy and have no balls; you must be a lawyer!!"

AFRICAN ROULETTE

65.

A diplomat from a somewhat obscure African country visits Moscow and is entertained at a lavish party with great huge amounts of food and vodka being consumed. Some reckless young officers, well into their cups, decide to give their guest a demonstration of the dangerous game known as "Russian Roulette", in which they explain, a revolver is loaded with one bullet only, then a man spins the cylinder, points the gun to his temple and pulls the trigger. If there is merely a click he wins that round and is considered very brave. If he happens to spin the cylinder to the loaded chamber then he is of course dead and is mourned as a brave man.

The African diplomat reciprocates with an invitation to his country which is accepted. Then after a lavish banquet thrown in honor of their guest the latter is presented by the host with six very naked and nubile young native girls. He is invited to pick one of the young ladies for a blow job. "This," the host says, "is is what we call 'African Roulette'."

The Russian is delighted with the prospect of getting a blow job from one of these buxom young ladies, and says, "Why do you call this 'African Roulette'?"

His host replies, "This game is loosely patterned after the game you showed me when I visited your country that you called, 'Russian Roulette'; in our game, one of the girls is a cannibal!"

THE DRUGGIST'S HELPER

66.

Picture, if you will…a one-man drugstore in a small town in Alabama. It's Saturday morning and the proprietor/druggist is there as is Leroy, the old black man who every Saturday morning comes in to sweep and dust the store. The phone rings, and the druggist answers it. The call is from a customer who wants a prescription delivered about a block away. Things are slow that morning, so after compounding the prescription in question, the druggist decides to deliver it himself.

As he leaves the store, he says, "Leroy, I'm going down the street; I'll be back in about ten minutes. Now, if the phone rings, you answer it, okay?" Leroy says, "Yassuh."

Sure enough no sooner than the druggist is out of there, the phone rings. Leroy picks it up and says, "Hullo!" The voice on the other end says, "Do you have any dihydroxymethylaminoethylolbenzine?" To which Leroy says, "Mistuh, when I said 'Hullo' I tole ya evrathin' ah knows 'bout dis bizniz!!"

SEEKING THE NEW IMAGE FROM
DR. WEINSTEIN

67.

Picture, if you will…a 28-year-old single girl who has been divorced for about six months. She decides that she is going to stop brooding and try to figure out how she can get back into the social swim, so to speak, and meet interesting people. She makes a self-appraisal of her assets. She has always been flat-chested and figures that if she were to have a fuller bust she might accomplish her goal as aforesaid. But she doesn't want surgery, and one of the girls at the office tells her, "Go see Dr. Weinstein, I understand that he feels as you do about surgery."

So she goes to see Dr. Weinstein and after listening to her thought says, "I believe as you do; I don't think surgery is the answer to the problem that you fancy you have. My program is quite simple, actually, and it is quite successful if faithfully followed: just put your hands together so that each hand is grabbing the fingers of the other hand and are thus interlocked in a tight grip, then pull hard with the muscles of your arms so that your hands are opposing each other in rhythm with the following ditty: 'Mary had a little lamb, its fleece was white as snow, and if I do this every day, my BOOBS are sure to grow'. On the word 'BOOBS' you should pull extra hard. This you should do each morning upon arising."

So our heroine faithfully does this exercise every morning when she gets up. One morning, however, she oversleeps and barely makes it to the bus. So she's sitting there and says to herself, "Oh, darn, I didn't do my exercise." She looks around the bus and sees that everyone else has their own little agendas, so she puts her hands together as prescribed and goes through the exercise saying the ditty to herself while tensing the proper muscles as instructed, "Mary had a little lamb...etc." Whereupon, a man seated behind her taps her on the shoulder and says, "You go to Dr. Weinstein, don't you?" She says, "Yes, do you know him?" "I sure do," he says, "Hickory dickery dock, a mouse ran up the clock, if I do this every day, I'll have a bigger..."

THE EMBARRASSMENT OF MONSIEUR DuPAIN

68.

Picture, if you will...a small cafe in Paris. Seated at ze bar is M'sieu DuPain. Lined up in front of him are six double cognacs; he is downing the second from the left. The proprietor of the establishment sees him thusly drinking and says, "M'sieu DuPain, why do you drink ze cognac like zis; always you drink ze wine?"

"Ah, moi foi! Eet ees terribl'; I came home early from a busines treep; I went to ze apartmanh of mah Suzette; I climbed ze stairs; I opened ze door wiz ze key weeth wheech she had provided me; I crossed ze living room to ze door to ze bedroom. What a sight! Ze moonlight was streaming through ze window and it fell upon ze beautiful white breasts of mah Suzette as zey rose and zey fell wiz her breathing; I was overcome! I bent down and keesed ze beautiful breasts of mah Suzette most passionately." Here, downing another cognac he continues, "Sacre bleu! Eet was not ze beautiful breasts of mah Suzette, but ze cheeks of ze ass of M'sieu DuVal!!!"

THE LAMENT

69.

Picture, if you will...two men seated at a bar having drinks. There seems to be a quasi-celebratory aspect to the occasion, and one says to the other, "Hey, Joe, how come you almost look happy tonight?

"Well, Harry, I was just thinking; if I had killed my wife twenty years ago like I wanted to, tonight I'd be a free man."

DOING THEIR BEADS

70.

Picture, if you will...the Cathedral at Milan. Giovanni and Giuseppe are kneeling there doing their beads. Giuseppe is on the aisle, and while thus engaged in religious activity he hears the sound of coins dropping on the tile floor across from him. He looks toward the source of the sound and sees a very pretty young girl stooping to retrieve the coins. And he sees that she has the most beautiful pair of ankles he has ever seen, and his gaze moves upward and he takes in the gorgeous well-rounder calves and the dimpled knees. He then notices that she is stylish attired in a micro miniskirt, so he lowers his head substantially so as to get a better look at her legs, and at this point Giovanni sees what is going on, and he gives his brother a stiff elbow in his side, saying, "Giuseppe! God is gonna strika you blind!!" With this, Giuseppe places a hand over his right eye, lowers his head even more and says, "I think I'ma gonna riska one eye!!!"

ABOUT MEN

71.

Men are what women marry. They have two hands, two feet and sometimes two wives, but never more than one idea at a time. Like Turkish cigarettes they are all made of the same materials; it's just that some are better disguised than others.

Generally speaking, men can be divided into two categories: husbands and unmarried men (bachelors, widowers and those who are divorced); for our purposes the three classes of unmarried men are interchangeable, so we can call the two classes "husbands" and "single men". A single man is an eligible mass of obstinacy entirely surrounded by women and a superabundance or, in fact glut, of experience. Husbands can be further divided into three sub-classes, prizes, surprises and consolation prizes. Making a husband out of a single man is the highest form of plastic art known to civilization. It takes science, sculpture, imagination, patience, faith, hope and charity…mostly charity.

It is a psychological marvel that a small, tender, sensitive and delicately-scented being like a woman should enjoy coming on to a big, awkward, stubble-chinned, cigar-smoking thing like a man.

If you flatter a man, you frighten him to death; if you don't, you bore him to death. If you permit him to make love to you right away, he gets tired of you in the end; if you don't, he gets tired of you in the beginning. If you believe everything he tells you, you soon cease to charm him; if you don't, he thinks you're playing with a short deck.

If you wear bright colors and startling hats, he hesitates to take you to out; but if you wear tailored suits and earth colors, he takes you out and spends the whole evening staring at women who are wearing bright colors and startling hats.

If you join him in gaieties and approve of his drinking, he swears that you are driving him to the devil; if you disapprove of his drinking and urge him to give it up, he vows that you are a party pooper.

If you are a clinging vine, he doubts whether you have a brain; if you are modern and intelligent, he doubts whether you have a heart. If you are silly, he longs for someone bright; if you are brilliant and intellectual, he longs for a playmate.

Man is just a worm in the dust. He comes along, wiggles around for a while, and then some chicken gets him!

THE TWO COSSAKS

72.

Picture, if you will...two Russian Cossaks galloping across the steppes of Russia on their trusty ponies; it's mid-winter, blizzard conditions. They arrive at a so-called comfort station which consists of nothing but a lean-to arrangement sheltering a galvanized steel trough. They alight to relieve themselves, and as they are standing there doing that, one says to the other, "Tell me, Boris, vy ees eet that ven you are pissink it sounds like the great vaterfall on the Volga near Pinsk as ze vater tumbles ofer ze precipice and crashes into ze gorge below, and ven I am pissink it sounds like the ze vater dripping off ze eaves into ze snowbank?"

"I tell you, Ivan, vy when I am pissink eet sounds like ze great vaterfall on ze Volga near Pinsk as ze vater tumbles over ze precipice and crashes into ze gorge below and ven you are pissink it sounds like ze vater dripping off ze eaves into ze snowbank; eet ees, Ivan, because I am pissink into zis galvanized steel trough, and you are pissink on my boots!!"

COLONEL SANDERS AND THE POPE

73.

Picture, if you will...the private audience chamber in the Vatican. Colonel Sanders is there with the Pope. The Colonel says, "Ah'm heah yo' holiness to tell ya that ah'm thinkin' of donatin' Five Million Dollahs to the church." "That would be very generous, my son," responds the Pope. Colonel Sanders goes on, "They's jes' one li'l condition, hy'evah; ya know that prayah y'll have that says, 'Give us this day ouah daily bread?' well, I want ya to change that a li'l bit so that it will say, 'Give us this day ouah daily chicken.'" "What?" says the Pope, "Tamper with the Lord's Prayer? There would be chaos in the Christian world!" "Well, how about ef'n ah made that Ten Million Dollahs?", says Col. Sanders. "Well, then I'd have to go into deep meditation and consult with the Cardinals."

So the Pope calls an assembly of the College of Cardinals, and after doing some serious meditating, he addresses them, "Gentlemen, I've been meditating over a proposition that has been presented to me, and I have good news and bad news. First the good news: we are going to receive a donation of Ten Million Dollars; the bad news is that we are losing the Pillsbury account."

<u>ONE DAY IN THE PARK</u>

74.

Recently, while walking through Bayfront Park, I encountered an elderly man sitting on bench who was weeping copiously. I said, "Excuse me, sir, you appear to be in great distress; is there anything that I can do to help?"

"I don't think so; I'm a man of seventy-nine years of age and three weeks ago I married a twenty-five-year old girl, and…" Here I interrupted him saying, "Stop right there; I know what the problem is: you can't keep up with her youthful sexual appetite."

"No, that's not it; she has carried me to new heights and has convinced me that there's nothing I can't do as far as sex is concerned." "Well, then," I said, "I think I know what it must be: you are a man who appears to me to be one who has traveled a great deal and dined in many of the finest restaurants; whereas, she is only 25 and probably can't even boil water."

"No, it's not that; she is a graduate of the Cordon Bleu School of Culinary Art is Paris; she serves me gourmet meals all the time." "Well, with all that great sex and gourmet eating, what makes you so unhappy?" To which the old gentleman said, "I can't remember where I live!!!"

<u>YOU'VE GOT TWO THINGS TO WORRY ABOUT</u>

75.

Come back with me to the Vietnam War era, and picture, if you will…a young man receiving from his postman a letter. He opens it; it starts, "GREETINGS FROM YOUR PRESIDENT…" It's a draft notice. Well, he's nervous, upset, anxious and excited and doesn't know what to do. Then he remembers that next door lives a retired Army Sergeant, so he take it over to him and says. "What do I do.?" The other says, "You read it and do what it says; next Thursday you go to the high school gym at 10:00 in the morning to take your physical.

"You've got two things to worry about: you flunk it or pass it. If you flunk it, you have nothing to worry about. If you pass it, you have two things to worry about: you get the Army or the Navy. If you get the Navy you've got nothing to worry about; if you get the Army you've got two things to worry about: you get Europe or Vietnam.

"If you get Europe, you've got nothing to worry about; if you get Vietnam, you've got two things to worry about: you get a desk job or a combat assignment. If you get a desk job, you've got nothing to worry about. If you get a combat assignment, you've got two things to worry about: you either get killed or you don't.

"If you don't get killed, you've not nothing to worry about; if you get killed you've got two things to worry about: they either make fertilizer or paper out of you.

"If they make fertilizer out of you you've got nothing to worry about; if they make paper out of you, you've got two things to worry about: they either make writing paper or toilet paper out of you.

"If they make writing paper out of you, you've got nothing to worry about; if they make toilet paper out of you, you have two things to worry about: they either put you in the men's john or the ladies' john.

"If they put you in the men's john, you've got nothing to worry about; if they put you in the ladies' john you've got two things to worry about."

WHEN YOU GOTTA GO

76.

Picture, if you will…the hallway outside a bathroom in a private residence; a party is in progress. A man is standing in front of the closed door; he knocks, and a voice comes from within, "Occupied."

He paces back and forth impatient to gain entry; he knocks again, and again he hears, "Occupied."

He paces some more and then knocks and says, "Hurry up, please; I've really got to go!" The occupant says, "Sorry; I'm not through yet."

The man waits a few minutes more, he can hardly stand it. He says. "Come on out, will ya; I'm about to drop a load in my pants!"

Then comes the reply, "Arrrrrrrrrnnnnnnnn't yooooooooooooou luuuuuuuuuuuucky!"

THE TUB AND THE DUCK

77.

Picture, if you will…a comely teenage country girl walking down a country road; she is carrying a tub. A nice-looking country lad is approaching from the other direction. He is carrying a duck. As they draw near to each other, the girl says, "Don't you dare seduce me, Charlie!" To which the lad replies, "Why, Sallie Lou, I have no intention of doing any such thing; besides, if I were to try anything like that I'd have to put my duck down and he'd get away, and he happens to be my favorite pet." So the girls says, "Well, I guess I could put this tub over him!!"

LORD CHUMLY-CHUMLY STAYS HOME

78.

Come with me to the estate of Lord Chumly-Chumly about 40 miles out of London. It is so vast in acreage that the railroad has built a station on the premises exclusively for him and his guests in return for a right-of-way.

One morning his chauffeur is driving him to the station so that His Lordship can take the 9:11 into London. However this plan is frustrated by a puncture.

The chauffeur fixes it as quickly as possible, but by the time they arrive at the station the train is disappearing around the bend.

"Oh, dash it all, I've missed my train; let's see, the next won't be along 'til eleven seventeen; by the time I would get into London the day would be jolly well half shot. I think I'll spend the day at home. Yes, that's what I'll do."

So he is driven back to his large mansion on the hill; he is going to tell Her Ladyship that he'll be spending the day at home. He enters the grand foyer, wends his way to the West wing, ascends the staircase to the second level and proceeds down the long hall to the door to the master bedroom suite to advise Lady Chumly-Chumly of his plans. There is Her Ladyship in bed...with the butler!

"Oh! My deah, this is most distressing! Of course divorce is the only solution. Well, you been a good wife, 'til now, and I shall be most liberal with you in the matter of the settlement, yes! You may have the townhouse in Park Lane; you may have the Rolls and the Mercedes; you may take Blaze and any of the other horses from the stable you may desiah; naturally you may have the furnichah. Oh! My deah, Couldn't you stop that while I'm speaking to you?!!"

THE WISDOM OF JESSE JACKSON

79.

Jesse Jackson is addressing a convention of white folks in Atlanta. He says, "You call me a 'colored man'; let's talk about that. When I was born I was born black. Now that I'm grown, I'm black. If I stay out in the sun too long, I'm still black. If I'm cold, I'm black. If I'm embarrassed, I'm black. If I get airsick or seasick, I'm black. When I die, I'll be black."

Then he picks out a man in the front row of the audience, and, focusing on him, says, "You are a white man. When you were born, you were pink. When you grew up, you were and are white. When you are cold, you are blue. When you are embarrassed or sunburned, you are red. If you get airsick or seasick, you get green. When you die, you'll be purple...and you call **ME** a colored man."

OLD FOLKS' HOME

80.

Picture, if you will...an Old Folk's Home. One of the little old ladies who resides there has developed a crush on one of the gentlemen residents. One day she approaches him and says, "Are you a bettin' man?"

He says, "Sometimes I'll bet; what you got in mind?"

She says, "I'll bet you ten bucks that I can tell you when you were born by fondlin' your genitals."

He says, "You're on; c'mon up to my room, and we'll see how good you are."

They go to his room and close the door. She Says, "Okay, drop your trousers and shorts." He does that, and she proceeds to fondle his genitals, very deliberately, finally saying, "You were born on August 25, 1908."

He says, "That's right. Fantastic! How do you do that?"

She replies, "You told me at breakfast the other day."

COLD HANDS

81.

The scene is the Province of Quebec, Canada, mid-winter, thirty below. A guy and a girl are in his car out on the highway; they are headed for a popular roadside restaurant; it's their first date. A tire goes flat; they are in the middle of nowhere with no cell phone, so he has to change the tire himself.

He has no gloves, so he has to do this task in spurts, so to speak. He gets out opens the trunk, takes out the spare and carries it over to the wheel where the problem is and then gets back in the car. His hands are freezing, so he says to his date; "This is a strange request on a first date, but would you mind if I put my hands between your thighs to warm them up?"

"No," she says, "this is after all, sort of an emergency." So he does that, and when his hands thaw out a little, he pops out of the car again and takes care of the next step in the process. Again and again he returns to the front seat and repeats the same hand-warming process, with his date's consent, of course.

Finally, she says to him when he gets in the car, "I have a question for you: don't your ears ever get cold?"

ARE YOU GETTING YOUR SHARE?

82.

The latest census figures indicate that there are approximately 260,000,000 people in the United States, of whom slightly more than one-half are females. Of this number (130,000,000), 3/8 or 48,750,000, are married and working at it.

The average length of the menstrual period is five days out of thirty, which means that 1/6 of these, or 8,125,000 are normally out of service on a given date. Marriage statistics show, however, that at least 50% of all married couples have intercourse during this period, notwithstanding the negative esthetic aspects of the situation, thus modifying the out-of-service figure to ½ to 4,062,500 for a serviceable total of 44,687,500.

It must be assumed that 25% of these are "just not in the mood tonight", thus eliminating an additional 11,171,875 to give a net serviceable total of 33,515,625.

The length of the penis during erection has been determined through exhaustive research to average five inches (despite considerable unsupported hearsay evidence that would tend to distort this statistic). The length of the stroke has been established at four inches, and married men are generally agreed that approximately 75 strokes are desirable before culmination. The product give us the figure of 300 inches which must be doubled (two-cycle operation) giving us the travel in relation to the vaginal wall.

Thus it is seen that 600 x 33,515,625 equals 20,109,375,000 inches, or 317,383 miles of penis being inserted and withdrawn every 24 hours. Furthermore, expressing these results in terms of miles-per-hour rate of travel, we see that the average rate of insertion and withdrawal (wall speed) is 13,244 miles per hour.

In other words, over 13,000 miles of penis are slipping in and out every hour of every day!

ARE YOU GETTING YOUR SHARE?

<u>THE ENTREPRENEUR</u>

83.

Picture, if you will…the kitchen in a mid-America farmhouse; it's a few days before Christmas, and the farmer is talking to his three young sons: "Boys, it's almost Christmas, and this year we can't afford to give you money for your presents, so I've decided to give each of you one of the farm animals; you can raise your animal or sell it or do anything with it you want…it'll be yours. Johnny, I'm going to give you a little lamb; Peter, I'm going to give you a little piggy, and Bobby, you get a duck. Now in a week, on Christmas day we'll all get together here and you can tell me what you have done with each of your animals."

At the scheduled time the farmer and his boys meet in the kitchen again. Johnny says that he has sold him lamb for $20.00, and his father compliments him for his success; then Peter tells them that he sold the piggy for $15.00, which is received with the approbation of his father. He then turns to Bobby and says, "Tell us, Bobby, what did you do with your duck?" At this Bobby holds up a fifty dollar bill, and his father is amazed. "Tell us how you were able to get so much money for the duck." And Bobby says, "Well, last night I headed for town with my duck under my arm, and it was raining and nasty, and a lady came along and picked me up and said I should come home with her and she would dry out my clothes and give me some hot chocolate. When we got to her house, she took my clothes and put them in the dryer and asked me about the duck, so I told her about it being my Christmas duck and all. The she said that if I would give her my duck she would take me to bed and do nice things with my body. So I said 'O.K.' and we did. Then a little while later she told me that if I'd do it again with her she would give me the duck back, so I did. By this time my clothes were dry, so I left with my duck and was on my way home, when a man driving a big car got forced off the road and almost hit me. In trying to get out of the way of the car I dropped the duck and the car ran over him and killed him. So the man got out and when he saw what had happened, he said, 'Oh, I'm sorry; I ran over your duck, and he probably was very important to you.' Then he gave me this fifty-dollar bill for my loss. So, I got a fuck for a duck, a duck for a fuck and fifty bucks for a fucked-up duck."

<u>SAVOIR FAIRE</u>

84.

Picture, if you will...a sidewalk cafe in Paris. Three Frenchmen and an American gentleman are conversing about this and that when the American says, "The English language as it is spoken today draws largely from other languages. The French language is no mean contributor, I might add. We use French words and phrases in our every-day speaking without bothering to translate them, because everyone seems to know what they mean and they are so apt in expressing a thought. Take, for example the phrase 'savoir faire'; you hear it often to describe a quality possessed by men of good taste, knowledge and experience." One of the Frenchmen steps in and says, "Ah! oui, 'savoir faire'; let me give you an example of what the term means to a Frenchman; a man comes home unexpectedly; he walks into the bedroom and his wife is in bed making love with anozzer man; he leaves the room without making his presence known; that is 'savoir faire'." The second Frenchman says, "Zat is close, Jacques, but I don't theenk zat zat is ze best example; let us use ze zame situation; ze man enters ze bedroom, he sees zem making love; he says, 'Continuez!'; he leaves; zat is 'savoir faire'." "No, no, Pierre; your example is bettair zan zat of Jacques; but I theenk it explains it bettair by taking your example a little bit further; he enters ze bedroom, he sees zem making ze love, he says, 'continuez'; he leaves; if ze ozzer man can continue, zat is 'savoir faire'!"

<u>HIS FIRST TRIAL</u>
<u>DISSOLUTION OF MARRIAGE</u>

85.

Picture, if you will...a young lawyer; it's his first trial: a divorce action. He has his client on the stand: a young, voluptuous, exotic lady; he is interrogating her about the material allegations of her complaint when, looking up at the Judge, he notices that the Judge is shuffling papers around, leafing through a volume, massaging his eyebrows; he doesn't think the Judge is paying attention, so he clears his throat rather loudly. The Judge looks up, looks over his half spectacles and looks down at the attorney; he says: "Yes, young man; what is it?" The young lawyer says, "This testimony is vital to my case; I was just hoping that you were getting it all." To which the Judge says, "Well, young man, I was listening; as I understand it, this is a divorce action; your client has charged her husband with extreme cruelty, and the gist of her testimony is to the effect that his penis is so large, that every time he attempts intercourse it's tantamount to rape; is that correct?" "Yes, Sir." "Well, young man, are you aware of the fact that your client was in here last year seeking a divorce from her then husband and charged him with extreme cruelty?" "No, Sir, I wasn't..." "Well, she was and she did, and I recollect that the gist of her testimony on that occasion was to the effect that *his* was so small that every time *he* attempted intercourse, it resulted in a monumental frustration. I want you to know, young man, that this Court has better things to do with its time than to try to fit precisely-proportioned peters to fussy pussies."

ZEBRA CURIOUSITY

86.

Picture, if you will...a zebra at the Pearly Gates seeking admission. He says to St. Peter, "Before I go in, I have a question that has been bothering me most of my adult life: am I a black zebra with white stripes or a white zebra with black stripes?"

St. Peter is stumped by the question and says, "I don't know; I'll have to ask GOD." So he leaves the scene to get the answer.

When he returns he tells the zebra that he asked GOD the question and GOD answered, "You are what you are." So, St. Peter says, "I guess that means that you are a white zebra with black stripes, because if you were a black zebra with white stripes GOD would have said, 'You iz what you iz!'"

THE KITTY HAWK

87.

Picture, if you will...the Kitty Hawk, one of our atomic-powered super aircraft carriers, one of the biggest ships in the world. A young lieutenant is piped aboard for duty and is immediately taken in tow by the Executive Officer (XO) who is to show him around the ship. They arrive at the Officers' Ward Room. XO says, "This is the ward room where we officers take our meals, relax, watch TV, write home, play cards and the like. Now today is Monday; I think you will like Monday night's menu: we have Sirloin steak, Caesar salad, apple pie a la mode."

The Lt. says, "Well, I don't eat meat, but the salad sounds good."

Then XO says, "Well, I think you will like Tuesday evenings; we have wine tastings with a variety of wines and cheeses." The Lt. says, "Well, alcohol does not pass between my lips, but I do like cheese."

Then the XO says, "I'm sure you're going to like Wednesday evenings; we bring out a bunch of young girls from the port and have an orgy here in the ward room." "Well," says the Lt., "I don't want to get involved with anything like that." To which the XO says, "Are you gay?" "Hell, no," replies the Lt. To which the XO says, "Well, then I don't think you are going to like Thursdays either!"

LEROY AND LIZA

88.

We have a black couple, Leroy and Liza; she wants children, and he doesn't, so he wears a condom when they do it. She says, "One of these days, ah'm gonna snatch that off and get pregnant." So Leroy starts wearing two condoms. Sure enough, one night she snatches off a condom and after they have completed a bout, she holds it high and says, "Aha, Leroy, mah man, now ah's prolly pregnant. Effen it's a boy weez gonna name him 'Leroy, Jr.', and' effen it's a girl, weez gonna name her 'Liza, Jr.'" At this, Leroy holds up the second condom and says, "An' effen he kin get outta heah, weez gonna call him 'Houdini'!!"

THE OLD MAN AND HIS FROG

89.

Picture, if you will...an 85-year-old man taking his constitutional one fine morning. He's passing a vacant lot that is sort of grown over with weeds. He hears a plaintive "Help me! Help me!", very faint. He searches through the weeds and finds a frog which is very happy at having been found, he says, "Thank you so much; you were nice enough to help me, so I am going to do something nice for you. If you'll kiss me I'll turn into a beautiful young woman who will forevermore be completely at your disposal; I'll do anything you want any time you wish." The old guy looks at the frog, thinks very briefly, and then puts the frog in his jacket pocket. Again he hears the "Help me!, Help me!", so he takes the frog out of his pocket, and the frog says, "I said, if you'll kiss me, I'll change into a beautiful young woman and do anything you like, and to clarify this point, it will mean great sex for you for the rest of your life!" The old man looks at the frog and says, "I understand what your saying, but at my age I think I'd rather have a talking frog."

MID-EAST EDUCATION

90.

Do you know why they don't teach sex education and drivers' ed on the same day in Saudi Arabia? Because it's too hard on the camels.

THE AVID GOLFER

91.

Picture, if you will...an avid golfer. He's getting married on Saturday at noon. He figures that he can get in nine holes in the morning and still get ready for the wedding in plenty of time, so he tells the bride, and she says, "OK but don't be late." So he goes to the club and moves right along until he gets to the ninth hole which is a little backed up from slow players ahead. There on the tee is a beautiful woman waiting for the fairway to clear for her drive. He says, "Do you mind if I play this last hole with you? I've only got a certain amount of time." She accedes to his wish as expressed and they play the ninth hole together, following which she says, "I like you; why don't we go over to my house and have a drink; I live right over there on the tenth fairway." He looks at his wristwatch and finds that he still has a little time and accepts her invitation. Well, one thing leads to another, and then they wind up in bed. By the time they are finished, he discovers that he's going to be late to his wedding, so he takes his leave, goes home, showers, puts on his wedding attire and rushes to the church. Well, no one is there except a somewhat irate minister, so he rushes over to the bride's parents' home where the reception has been scheduled, and there is the bride and she is conspicuously upset and weeping a little. He decides to tell her the whole story and says that he met this beautiful woman who took him home and made love to him and he was unable to resist because he's weak. Whereupon, she says, "Now, "Don't lie to me, you bastard, you played eighteen."

THE PARATROOPER

92.

A Vietnam veteran paratrooper decided that his son should follow in his footsteps and become a paratrooper also, so he drummed it into him right from small childhood, and this was effective, and the boy joined the army and volunteered for the paratroops, although he really had no enthusiasm for the concept and was only doing it to please his dad. So, a propos to this the young man is sitting in a bar with a good friend of his and the following dialogue ensues:

YPT: So there I was up in a C-117 programmed to make my first jump. I fastened my parachute release hook to the wire and approached the door. Well, I froze; I couldn't do it, and I told the jump master, a sergeant, that I changed my mind and didn't want to do it. The jump master said, 'Either you jump and right now, or I'm going to strip down your pants and bugger you right here and now!'

GUY: "Did you jump?"

YPT: "Well, yes, a little…at first."

THE PRIDE OF GILLETTE

93.

A young lady who worked in the Gillette razor blade factory inadvertently swallowed a razor blade. On the way down it gave her a tonsillectomy, a hysterectomy, an appendectomy, circumcised her boy friend, cut off the finger of a chance acquaintance, sheared off the Rabbi's beard…and she still had 12 shaves left.

THE INDICTMENT

94.

A man we know was indicted for the crime of bestiality, and the essence of the charge was that he allegedly had intercourse with a goat. So he thought he'd better get a lawyer. He interviewed a couple of criminal lawyers who quoted very substantial retainers. He couldn't afford what they asked, so he made inquiries and talked with a young lawyer at the suggestion of a friend who said he thought that the attorney's fee would be more reasonable…something he might live with. The lawyer in question told him quite candidly that he had very little experience with criminal matters but added that people said that he had a real knack for picking a jury…and his fees were reasonable. So he hired him, he picked a jury and they went to trial.

The prosecutor put his first witness on the stand and asked him: "Where were you on August 17th at 3:30 PM?" The witness replied, "I was behind farmer Brown's barn." "Did you see anything unusual at that time and place?" "Yes, I did; I saw a man having intercourse with a goat!" "Is that man in the courtroom today?" "Yes, he is; that man sitting right over there." (Indicating the defendant.) "After that act was completed did you see anything else which you would consider unusual?" "Yes, I did; after the act was completed, the goat turned around, came back to the man and licked his privates." At this point, one of the jurors turned to his neighbor and whispered behind his hand, "A good goat'll do that!"

MIDDLE-AGED MARRIAGE

95.

This middle-aged couple met, fell in love and got married. It's their wedding night; they are in the honeymoon suite of the Plaza. As she gets into bed, she says, "I hope you will be gentle with me; I'm still a virgin." "What do you mean you're still a virgin? You told me yourself that you have been married three times before. What's the story here?" To which she replies, "My first husband was a gynecologist, and all he wanted to do was look at it. My second husband was a supply-side economist, and all he did was tell me how good it was going to be. My third husband was a stamp collector, and all he wanted to do was …**OH!!! HOW I MISS THAT MAN!!!"**

FIRST GOOD NEWS/BAD NEWS JOKE

96.

Picture, if you will…The Garden of Eden. God has just created Adam. HE tells him that he is going to pluck a rib from his side and create a woman for him who will be named Eve and explains that he and Eve have been chosen to initiate the procedure that will result in the Earth's being populated. HE says to Adam, "First I have to tell you that I have good news for you and bad news; first the good news: in order for you and Eve to do this and have fun at the same time I am going to furnish the two of you with something called SEX. This is an essential part of the procreation process, but its chief function is to take you and Eve to great heights of ecstasy beyond your wildest imaginings! That's the good news; now for the bad news, 'I'm putting woman in charge!'"

STATE OF THE ART, TOP OF THE LINE

97.

Picture, if you will…a lady who has just fulfilled a longstanding wish: she has purchased and is driving away from the agency in the most expensive Mercedes sedan made. She turns on the radio and hears something that does not interest her, so she fiddles with some knobs and pushes some buttons, but nothing happens. So she does a quick 180 and goes right back to the agency and searches out the salesman that handled the transaction with her. She says, "Tell me how much I paid for this car." And the other replies, "$132,500, plus tag, title and tax." "Well," she says, "Don't you think I should have a radio that actually works?" "Oh," says the salesman, "I guess you didn't get checked out on your radio; it's state of the art, cutting edge, it's voice activated." "What do you mean?" she says. "Well, if you want to hear country music for example, you just say 'Country' and the radio will find you country music, or jazz or rock and roll, whatever."

So, she leaves and while proceeding along the way she decides to try out this special radio, so she says, "Country", and sure enough out of the ten speakers of this exceptional system comes Willie Nelson singing his latest. She is impressed and says, "Jazz", and immediately the radio finds Dave Brubeck and his quartet. Then she says, "Rock and Roll", and hears one of the Beatles' greats. Just then some reckless fool cuts right in front of her, and she hollers, "Ass hole!", and the radio switches right over to Clinton's press conference.

TWO-LINERS

98.

What is the difference between chicken and meat? Ans. If you beat your chicken, it will die.

What do you get when you cross a donkey with an onion? Ans. Sometimes you get an onion with long floppy ears, but once in a while you get a piece of ass that brings tears to your eyes.

THE CHANGING OF THE GUARD
AT BUCKINGHAM PALACE

99.

Picture, if you will…the changing of the guard at Buckingham Palace. It's a special event, and the Queen is there. After one group of troopers have been replaced and are out in the dispersal area, the Sgt. Major places one of them in a stiff brace, his nose a mere three inches away from that of the S/M.   The following colloquy takes place:

St. Major: Smithby, did I see you wince as Her Majesty went by?
Smithby: Yes, sah!
S/M: What is your excuse, Smithby?
Smithby: No excuse, sah, but I have an explanation.
S/M: An explanation, Smithby; what do you mean?
Smithby: Well, sah, as the Queen was approaching, a squirrel ran up my left trouser leg and lodged himself in the area of my crotch.
S/M: Oh, is that when you winced, Smithby?
Smithby: No, sah. Following that incident another squirrel ran up my right trouser leg and lodged himself in the same area.
S/M: Oh, is that when you winced, Smithby?
Smithby: No sah.
S/M: **When did you wince, Smithby?**
Smithby: I winced, sah, when one said to the other, "Let's eat one now, and save the other for the Winter."

THE QUEEN'S TRIP TO EDINBURGH

100.

The Queen was scheduled to make a trip to Edinburgh, all very official. She sends her personal envoy, a Brigadier, up one month in advance, so everything will be set up according to protocol. Part of the Queen's welcoming ceremony involves her reviewing a crack Scottish regiment dressed in their kilts and all.

On the occasion of the initial inspection of the regiment by the Brigadier, he is going down through the ranks and comes to one soldier who has a very decided tilt to his kilt. He takes the Sgt. Major aside and says, "I say, we cawn't have this sort of thing; I suggest that you give that chap a week-end pass." "Yes, sor," says the Sgt. Major.

Two weeks later the Bridagier comes by for his second inspection to assure himself that everything is progressing smoothly; he comes to the same soldier, and again there is a similar manifestation. The Brigadier is visibly shaken and takes the Sgt. Major aside and says, "Did you give that chap a week-end pass as I suggested?" "Yes, sor." "Well" says the Brigadier, "We cawn't take the chance with the Queen coming and all; I suggest you give him a week in London; we've got the time!"

On the day before the Queen is scheduled to arrive, the Brigadier comes back for his final inspection, to see that all the loose ends are tied up and everything is letter-perfect, and he finds that the same soldier again has a tilt to his kilt. He is incensed, and rightly so. He takes the Sgt. Major aside and says, "Did you give that chap a week in London, as I suggested?" "Yes, sor," replies the Sgt. Major. "Well," says the Brigadier, "why cawn't he control himself?" "Biggin' your pardon, sor, it appears that he's tykin' quite a lykin to ye!"

THE WEDDING NIGHT

101.

Picture, if you will...the bridal suite of the George Cinc Hotel in Paris. The occupants are a newly-wed couple. He is French, and she is an American girl; they have known each other a very short time...a whirlwind romance. She puts on her filmiest nightgown, very lacy, very sexy, and gets into bed. The groom returns from the bathroom and kneels down beside the bed. This evokes a comment from his bride, "Jacques, I did not know you were so religious as to say your prayers by the bed before joining me here." To which Jacques replies, "Ma cher, I am not ze religious fanatic that I may appear to be...actually Jacques is merely saying grace!"

THE YOUNG LAWYER

102.

Picture, if you will...a young lawyer who has in tow his girl friend; he is showing her around the courthouse so she will know what he does when he's doing his lawyer bit and have a better idea how the courts operate. There is a trial in progress wherein the defendant is accused of indecent exposure. The defendant is on the stand being cross examined by the D.A. when he whips out his hoo-hoo and starts beating it vigorously. The girl friend is shocked and dismayed and says, "Why this is terrible...he shouldn't be doing that !!" "You're absolutely right, my dear, says the young lawyer, "he's getting finger prints all over Exhibit A."

THE DIRTY BIRD

103.

A middle-aged spinster lady has just bought a parrot at the local pet shop to keep her company; she lives alone. The proprietor has guaranteed to the customer that the bird will talk. The next scene is her apartment; she removes the cover from the cage, and the parrot looks at her and says, "Hey, Baby, how about a little sex?" She is shocked, disturbed and upset by this. Unfortunately the parrot keeps repeating the same offensive question, so she covers the cage to silence him. She then calls her pastor and spiritual advisor for comfort and guidance.

The minister says that he thinks he has a solution to the problem. It seems that he has two pious lady parrots who pray a lot and frequently quote from the scriptures. He suggests that she bring her bird over to his place saying that if her bird were to be exposed to his pious birds perhaps some of it would rub off on him.

So she does that; she takes the bird to her pastor's home and puts the bird in the cage with his two pious parrots. Her bird looks at the two lady parrots and says, "Hey, ladies, how about some sex?" One of the pastor's parrots cocks her head and says to the pastor's second parrot, "At last our prayers have been answered."

THE FRENCH/USA DAVIS CUP TIE

104.

Picture, if you will…a banquet the evening prior to the French/USA Davis Cup Tie scheduled to commence the next day in the stadium on Key Biscayne. The scene is The Grand Bay Hotel in Coconut Grove, Miami, Fla. Butch Buchholz, the genius behind the state-of-the-art, cutting-edge stadium on Key Biscayne, and host for the evening is seated with four French players. He turns to one and says, "Are you married, Pierre?" and when the answer comes back in the affirmative, Butch ventures further, "Do you have any children?" To which the other replies, "No, unfortunately, eet ees eempossible; you see, sir, my wife, she ees, how you says?…**inconceivable**." At this point another of the Frenchmen interrupts and says, "M'sieu Buchholz, you weel haf to forgeeve Pierre; he does not speek zee Eengleesh so well; what he meant to say was zat hees wife, she ees **impregnable**.".

At this, a third member of the French team says, "René, I theenk zat what you weeshed to say to our host was not what you said; like Pierre, your Eengleesh leaves somzing to be desired." Then turning to Butch he says, "What Pierre actually meant to say was zat hees wife, she ees **unbearable**." With this the fourth Frenchman says, "M'sieu Buchholz, you must forgeeve my colleagues, zey do not have so good zee Eengleesh; Jacques and René were as bad as Pierre een trying to explain to you why Pierre has no cheeldren…what zey all meant to say was zat Pierre's wife, she ees **inscrutable**."

THE LITTLE GIFT

105.

Picture, if you will…an elegant cocktail lounge; seated at the bar is a svelte and stylish lady. A thirty-fivish out-of-town gentleman, quite handsome, takes the stool next to hers and engages her in conversation. One thing leads to another; there is a palpable plenitude of electricity between them, and after a few drinks and dinner he follows her to her tastefully-appointed apartment, and, after a nightcap they wind up in bed for a mutually-satisfying night of concentrated passion and reckless abandon. Over breakfast in the morning he very adroitly inquires of the lady what sort of a present he might thrust upon her for such a memorable night, diplomatically expressing the hope that she will not be offended by the suggestion. She says that she is not one to take umbrage at such an offer and tells him that he could favor her with an eight-bladed, gold-plated, pearl-handled pocket knife which conveniently is available at a nearby store. He departs and returns with the knife she described, she thanks him and he leaves.

About two months later business brings him to the same city, so he gives her a call. She accepts his invitation to dinner, and, as he had hoped, they spent the night making love as before. He can't believe his good fortune and again brings up the subject of what sort of gift she might like as memento of the beautiful experience. She says that she would really only like another eight-bladed, gold-plated, pearl-handled pocket knife, which he obtains with alacrity.

As you might imagine, his curiosity is aroused by the repetitive nature of the unusual gift that seemed to please her so much and asks her why she wanted just that item twice. She says that she likes him a lot and would tell him what is behind this wish for the second knife, and then opens one of her bureau drawers which is full of eight-bladed, gold-plated, pearl-handled pocket knives. He is astounded and asks why this passion for that one object. She explains, "Well, I'm young now and am considered a very beautiful and desirable woman; I have no trouble finding handsome and compatible men like you with whom to enjoy the pleasures of sex. But, the day will come when my looks and desirability fade…I've got to face that. When that time arrives, can you imagine what a boy would do for me for an eight-bladed, gold-plated, pearl-handled pocket knife?"

AT THE ZOO

106.

A lady of very dignified demeanor is visiting the zoo; She stops by the cages housing the porcupines. On her left is a cage labeled, "South African Porcupine", and next to it is one labeled "North American Porcupine". She looks back and forth between the two and perceives no difference between them. So she snags a zoo attendant and asks him, "What is the difference between these two types of porcupines; they look the same to me."

"Well," he says, "The South African Porcupine has a prick that is six inches long, and the other has a prick that is ten inches long. That's about it."

The lady is incensed, her delicate sensibilities have been offended, so she goes to the office of the Superintendent of the Zoo to make a complaint. "This man was terribly vulgar to me," she says, "He should be fired!" "What did he say, Madam; his exact words?" So she reluctantly tells him verbatim; it's all she can do to get the words into and out of her mouth.

After she has finished with her recital, he says, "Try not to get so upset, lady; it's obviously a mistake. What he meant was that the *quill* of the South African Porcupine is six inches long and the *quill* of the North American Porcupine is ten inches long. Lady, there isn't a porcupine in the whole world that has a prick ten inches long."

<u>BUGS IN ZE BUSHES</u>

107.

Picture, if you will...a doctor's office. A very cute and chic, but dejected, French lady comes in. The doctor says, "What can I do for you, little lady?" "Oh, docteur, eet ees terribl'; I haf ze bugs in ze bushes and I do not know what to do for zem; perhaps you haf zumzing zat you can gif me, non?"

"Well," says the doctor, "what we are talking about here is the crab louse. You can relax; during World War II the army developed a powder that is very effective against this bug. I'm going to give you a can of this powder; you follow the directions on the can and come back in a week and tell me if it has been effective, okay?" "Oh, merci, docteur," she says, and leaves.

A week later she comes back and appears to be in good spirits. In answer to his question concerning the effectiveness of the powder, she says, "Oh, oui, docteur; magnifique!! No more ze bugs, but, no more ze bushes, and Pierre's moustache, POOF!!!"

<u>THE OBSCENE TELEPHONE CALL</u>

108.

Picture, if you will...a remote telephone booth. In the booth is a pervert who gets his kicks by making obscene phone calls. He has his victim all picked out and has enough coins for three calls, for security. He puts in some coins, dials and gets a busy signal; he hangs up; the phone is defective and steals his coins. He puts in more coins and dials; he gets the wrong number; that man hangs up, and again he loses his coins. So now he is down to his last coins. He checks the number again, deposits his coins and dials very carefully. He is cautiously elated when he hears the phone ringing.

A little girl picks up the phone and says, "Hello." "Hello, little girl," he says, "is your mommy there?" "No, Mommy's not here," she replies. "Okay," says the sex fiend, "Then let me talk to your baby sitter," "I don't have a baby sitter," says the little girl. To this the man says, "How old are you, little girl?" "I'm four years old," she says. "You're four years old, and you're there all by yourself?" he says. "Yes," she says, "are you there all by yourself, too?" "Yes, as a matter of fact I am," he says. To which she says, "Doo-doo, poopy, tinkle."

<u>THE LAST SUPPER</u>

109.

    Q. What were the last words said at The Last Supper?

    A. "Separate checks, please!"

THE HIGH RISE APARTMENT

110.

Picture, if you will…a man and a woman in bed in a high rise apartment building. They are doing it, but they're not married to each other. Their enthusiasm for what they are doing is palpable, but while thus engaged they suddenly hear a key sort of rattling in the front door lock. The man says, "My God, who's that?" "That must be my husband," she says, "but he wasn't due back until tomorrow; quick, jump out the window!" "Are you crazy?" he says, "This is the thirteenth floor!" To which she says, "This is no time to be superstitious!!!"

TOO MANY CHILDREN

111.

Picture, if you will…a black doctor's office. A man has just come in to see the doctor. "Wus wrong you think ah kin he'p ya?" says the doctor. "Well, doctor," he says. "iss lak diss: ah's got fi' kids an mah woman done got pregunt agin. I cain't affo'd to hav enny mo' kids; dass it; kin ya he'p me?"

So the doctor pulls down from the shelf a very large book and says, "Lessee whut the medical volume sez 'bout dis; ah thinks you mus' be suff'rin from potency; les look at dat. Ah, heah tiz; de book say 'If de patient is suff'rin fum "Potency" the cuah us to remove one of the testiclees;' lest hack dat off, Boy!" And so he does.

Many months later the same man is back in the office with a similar complaint; his wife had that baby and is pregnant again. The doctor says, "Lessee, you was suff'rin fum 'potency' as ah recollects; les fahnd out what de medical volume say about dis sitcheeation; heah 'tiz, de book say that if the cuah fo' 'potency' is ineffective the patient may be suff'rin fum 'supah potency'; lessee what the book sez undah dat; ah heah 'tiz; it say, 'Effen de patient is suff'rin fum "supah potency", de cuah is to remove de othah testiclee;' les take dat off." And he does.

Many months later the man returns to the doctor with a substantially similar complaint, so the doctor hauls down the medical volume and opens to "super potency", because that's what he had diagnosed on his last visit. "Ah," says the doctor, "heah we got 'supah potency', and dey iz a askerisk heah; dat mean dey iz a footnote of sum kahnd. Heah 'tiz, 'If the cuah fo' super potency is ineffective, you done cut the balls offen de wrong niggah!!'"

HARD TIMES

112.

Picture, if you will…a strip shopping center. A new two-story building has just been finished and the tenants move in. There are three tenants upstairs and three on the ground floor, arranged as follows:

DENTIST	DANCE STUDIO	CAT HOUSE
PHARMACY	BEAUTY PARLOR	HARDWARE

After six months one of the tenants goes bankrupt. The riddle is: Which goes bankrupt, and why?

The answer: The hardware store goes bankrupt, because they couldn't stand the fucking overhead.

SHADES OF THE BARD

113.
Look at the following diagram and then tell me which of Shakespeare's plays each of the squares represents:

WET	DRY	MISCARRIAGE
4"	6"	8"

Upper left: Midsummer's Night's Dream; Upper middle: 12th Night; upper right: Love's Labor Lost; Lower left: Much Ado About Nothing; Lower middle: As You Like It; Lower right: Taming of the Shrew.

114.
NEXT MONTH IS…

NATIONAL CONDOM MONTH

THE SLOGANS ARE…

1. Cover your stump before you hump.
2. Before you attack her, wrap your whacker.
3. When in doubt, shroud your spout.
4. You can't go wrong if you shield your dong.

5. If you're not going to sack it, go home and whack it.
6. If you think she's spunky, cover your monkey.
7. She won't get sick if you wrap your dick.
8. If you go into heat, packiage your meat.
9. Never deck her with an uncovered pecker.
10. Wrap your foil before checking her oil.
11. A crank with armour will never harm her.
12. Don't be a fool, vulcanize your tool.
13. Don't be a prick, saran wrap your dick.
14. If you slip between her thighs, please be sure to condomize.

THE CHANDELIER

115.

Picture, if you will…a convent high in the mountains; a young probationary nun, or novitiate, as they call them, has been assigned the task of cleaning the 600-year-old crystal chandelier, the pride and joy of the institution; with hundreds of multi-faceted pendants. She was up on a high step ladder with her Windex and a chamois skin and had cleaned all she could reach, so she started to climb down and move the ladder over so that she could cover a new area. On the way down the ladder a catastrophe occurred: her foot caught in the hem of her vestment, and she started to fall. Instinctively she reached out and grabbed the chandelier which from the added weight of her person broke loose and crashed to the floor shattering into smithereens. The novitiate quickly surveyed the scene and said, "Oh shit! Oh God Dammit, I said 'Shit', oh shit, I said 'God Dammit'; oh fuck it; I didn't want to be a nun anyway!"

DUCKING THE ISSUE

116.

Picture, if you will…a very upscale grocery store; a lady who is in there for the first time asks to meet the store manager and announces that she and her family have just moved in Miami in connection with her husband's appointment as new CEO of his company. She says that she has heard of the store's marvelous reputation and she wants to establish an account with them. The store manager says that he will be delighted to have her as a new customer and that she may be assured that she will receive the best attention; further that they sell nothing but the best quality of everything. She thanks him and says, "For my first purchase, I'd like a nice Long Island Duckling." The store manager says that he will handle this order personally and goes back into the butcher department returning with a duck that he places on the counter. The lady then takes the index finger of her right hand, inserts in into the cloaca of the duck and moves it all around, finally announcing, "this isn't a Long Island Duck; this bird is from Louisiana." "I'm dreadfully sorry, Madam; there has been a mix-up of some sort; I'll get you the proper duck." He is gone for a few minutes and returns with a new duck, which she examines internally in the same thorough manner, announcing that this one is from New Jersey. They go through the same routine twice more before the lady is satisfied that she finally has a Long Island Duck. The manager thanks the lady for her patience and says the matter has been quite embarrassing and he so wanted to make a good impression on a lady whom he wanted to be a regular customer. The lady is impressed by the charm and grace of the man and says, "You are a very gracious shopkeeper, and I will be back to deal with you in the future; by the way, where are you from?" With this, the store manager turns around, drops his trousers, bends over spreads his cheeks and says, "Madam, you're the expert; you tell me."

THE VIRGIN BRIDE

117.

Picture, if you will...the honeymoon suite of the Waldorf Astoria in Manhattan. Ensconced therein is a newly-nuptialized and very handsome young couple. He is the scion of a wealthy Italian family that boasts eminent antecedents. It is a requirement that before a male member of the family can take a bride she must swear on everything holy that she is a virgin. She has so sworn and the wedding was beautiful.

The couple prepares for bed and lovemaking ensues. The girl is such a marvelous lover that her husband entertains vague doubts about her virginity. He says, "You, my darling, give me the utmost of pleasure from the perfection of your techniques, but it also gives me great pain in that I find it difficult to think that you could be a virgin and know so much about sexual matters."

The bride says, "Do not have pain, my husband, and be ever assured that I was a virgin when I came to this bed. I learned about sex in the convent in Switzerland where I spent the last four years.

"You learned all those wonderful movements in a convent? I find that hard to imagine. How can you learn all that in a convent where there is no sex at all, presumably? I want to believe you, and the blood on the sheets certainly supports what you say, but your technique...it is most puzzling."

With this on the table, so to speak, the bride relates the following, "I'll tell you all about it. The last year of my matriculation at the convent school, the Mother Superior taught a course in marital sex, for it is a cornerstone of that school that young ladies that graduate therefrom will be well-prepared for life in general and marriage in particular, recognizing that sex is an important aspect of married life.

"In the first lesson on sexual technique, the Mother Superior gave each of us girls an apple tied to a long ribbon, instructing us to hang the ribbon over our right shoulder across our body so that the apple rested against our left hip. She had us each practice the proper movement as she said, 'Bump the apple, bump the apple.'

"The next lesson involved a pear also on a long ribbon which we were to hang over our left shoulder across our bodies so that the pear was resting on our opposite hip. So it was then 'Bump the apple, touch the pear; bump the apple, touch the pear.'

"The third lesson involved a banana hanging on a ribbon and so placed that it hung between our little buns, Then it was, 'Bump, the apple, touch the pear and hit the banana; bump the apple, touch the pear and hit the banana.'

"And the last lesson involved the hanging of a small bag of coffee beans designed to hang down in front of our little virgin pussies. Then it was, 'Bump the apple, touch the pear, hit the banana, and **GRIND THE COFFEE!!**'"

THE FREUDIAN SLIPS

118.

Picture, it you will…the waiting room in a psychiatrist's office. Two men are sitting there, and they start talking to each other. One says to the other, "If you don't mind my asking, what brings you to a psychiatrist's office?" The other replies. "I don't mind your asking. Yesterday I committed a very embarrassing freudian slip. I was in the airline's ticket office. The girl behind the counter had a tremendous mammarial development, and when she asked me what she could to for me I said, 'I want a round trip picket to Titsburgh.' So, I thought I'd could stand a little analysis." The other then said, "Well, strangely enough, I'm here because I too committed a very embarrassing freudian slip; it was this morning; I was having breakfast with my wife, and I meant to say, 'Please pass the Cheerios.' but instead I said 'You rotten bitch; you've ruined my life!'"

THE COMPUTER SPEAKS

119.

Picture, if you will…a very modern up-to-date employment office with chrome and leather furniture and a state-of-the-art computer adapted to the needs of this business with the latest software. In walks a thirtyish black fellow, nice-looking, well-groomed and beautifully dressed. He says, "I've come here to find a position that will take the greatest advantage of my potentialities, capabilities and aptitudes." The young lady assigned to serve him says, "You have come to the right place, just give me your background information and I will feed it into the computer which will then tell us what you are best suited for." He did and she did and in 3 ten-thousandths of a second the printer started whirring and the printout emerged. It looked like this:

BIMM
HY

B A R
T P C T

The applicant looked at the printout and said, "I think I know what that say: it means that I am going to Bimini and get a high paying job in a bar, but I doan know why I'd need a topcoat in Bimini." The young lady says, "No, no, no! You've got that all wrong; what it says is, *"Be in Memphis Monday; have your black ass ready to pick cotton Tuesday.*

THE MEANING OF FEATHERS

120.

Picture, if you will…a small Native American Indian village in Arizona. A young anthropologist student is doing some research for her master's degree. She sees an Indian brave who is wearing one feather in his head band. She explains to him why she is there and asks him what the one feather in his head band means. He replies, "Uunh! Wear one feather, screw one squaw." She writes that down and continues on her way.

She encounters a brave that is wearing two feather in his head band, and he tells her that he wears two feathers, because he screws to squaws.

Next she sees the Chief; he has a magnificent headdress full of feathers all the way to the ground. She approaches him, tells him what she is doing in their village and asks him what all the feathers mean.

He replies, "Uuunnnh! Screw all squaws, got all feathers!" As she is making a note on this she mutters, "Hostile!" He hears her and says, "Hoss style, dog style, all style, any style!" And she, still writing, says, "Oh dear!" To which the Chief responds, "No deer; stand too all, move too fast!"

GOLF IS A DANGEROUS GAME

121.

Picture, if you will…a proctologist's office. A man with a putter stuck up his ass is being attended to by the doctor. The doctor is naturally a mite curious concerning the circumstances surrounding the insertion of the golf club and asks, "Tell me, how on earth did you get into this predicament anyway." "Well," he says, "it was a poor choice of words I guess. I was out playing golf with my wife. We were on the second green, both lying three. I was away and putted my ball; I rimmed the cup and then tapped it in. Then my wife putted and dropped a 20 foot putt right in the middle of the cup. I stooped to retrieve her ball and made the critical mistake of saying, "This looks like your hole, dear." Right then she let me have it.

WHERE'S THE GUGGENHEIM?

122.

Picture, if you will…a Pakistantian gentleman on the sidewalk on Central Park East in Manhattan. He is well dressed, nicely groomed. He has put up with urban manners for some weeks and has become used to how things are handled in the city. He approaches a citizen who is walking down the sidewalk and says, "Excuse me, sir, but could you please direct me to the Guggenheim Museum, or should I just go fuck myself?"

THE QUIZ SHOW

123.

Picture, if you will…a TV quiz show set. A lady contestant is about to be quizzed by the quiz-master. He says to her, "If you answer correctly three questions, the trip for two to Hawaii is yours. First question: What do you call a man that kisses another man all over?" "A homosexual", she answers. "Correct. Now what do you call a woman who kisses another woman all over?" "A lesbian," she says. "Again, correct; now for the last question, and remember, if you answer this one correctly, the trip is yours. What do you call a man who kisses a woman all over?" "Well," she says, "I don't know the technical term, but I'd call him 'Darling'".

THE HOO-HOO VS. THE TAIL OF THE CAT

124.

The scene is the local pub. An habitué with a snoot full is involved with another patron in a discussion, concerning the claimed superior dimensions of the former's male caudle appendage. The drunk, wishing to settle the matter once and for all says, "See that cat over there? Well I'll bet you ten bucks that my hoo-hoo is longer than that cat's tail." The bet was accepted and they enlisted the bartender to take the measurements and announce the winner. When the dust had settled, the bartender announced that the patron's hoo-hoo was a smashing 7½" in length, but the cat's tail edged him out at 8¼"; whereupon, the bettor claimed the stakes. "Jush a minute," says the drunk to the bartender, "would you be kind enuff to tell me from what point you measured the cat's tail?" The bartender replies, "From his anus to the tip, of course." The drunk then rejoined, "I thought so; would you mind extending me the same courtesy?"

THE GREATEST LOVE

125.

There's the wonderful love of a beautiful maid,
And the love of a staunch, true man,
And the love of a baby unafraid
Has existed since time began.

But the greatest love, the love of loves,
Greater than that of a mother,
Is the tender, passionate, infinite love
Of one drunken bum for another.

THE FRENCH LUAU

126.

That's where the men screw the pigs and eat the women.

THE SPECIMEN

127.

A man went in to see the doctor about his arm that was hurting. The waiting room was full, and the nurse/receptionist said that the doctor was so busy that it was impossible for him to get to see him. She handed him a specimen bottle and suggested that it might expedite matters if he would bring back a urine specimen the next morning, to start with, stating that she would do what she could to work him in. Well, he was mad at being brushed off, so when he came in the next day with the specimen bottle it contained samples of his urine, his wife's, his daughter's, his dog's and his neighbor's. Again the nurse said that the doctor was too busy to work him in that day, but she promised that she would phone him with the results of the urine test in a few hours.

About two hours later, true to her word, the nurse calls him and says, "We have the report from the lab about your specimen, and here's what it says: Your wife has a social disease that she contracted from your neighbor; your daughter is pregnant, your dog has worms, and if you don't stop playing with yourself, you'll get a sore arm."

THE PRACTICAL SOLUTION

128.

A socially and politically prominent English couple, he a member of the House of Lords, appeared at the office of a surgeon of their long acquaintance with the news that their 17-year-old daughter was pregnant. They said it would be ruinous for their daughter to give birth out of wedlock and beseeched him to perform an abortion. He said that the ethics of his profession would not allow him to do that, but he added, "I have a plan that will solve everything: the Archbishop of Henly will shortly have to undergo an appendectomy. When your daughter starts having labor pains, let me know and I shall make the necessary arrangements."

As soon as the labor pains started the doctor installed the girl in one operating room and the Archbishop in an adjoining one. He delivered the baby and removed the appendix. He then took the child into the presence of the archbishop, who was just coming out of the effects of the anesthesia and said

"Your Grace, it wasn't your appendix after all; it was a miracle, and this is your son!"

The Archbishop, a devoutly religious man, accepted the story of the miraculous birth and raised the boy as his own. He turned out to be a fine handsome young man, and when he was about 25 years of age, one day the Archbishop, who was on his deathbed, called him into his room and said, "Son, there is something that I have to tell you before I die. I should have told you years ago, but I kept putting it off." "What is it? Father", interrupted the boy. "That's just it, Son, I'm not your father; I'm your mother...the Vicar of Wakefield is your father!"

THE LATEST GOLFING ATTIRE

129.

A golf fiend we know showed up on the first tee the other day to greet the members of his usual foursome. One of the group noticed that he had a large round hole in the rear of his pants and a matching hole in his undershorts, both neatly stitched. Inquiry was made by the guys as to what this was all about, and he replied, "Well, it has several advantages, actually; first of all, these pants used to be a little tight and constricting, now, with this feature they are looser and more flexible, and I have more ball room. Secondly, you can readily appreciate the air conditioning aspects of this hole; the breeze blows right through and cools me off. Thirdly, moreover, and most importantly, it keeps the gnats out of my eyes when I'm putting."

THE PROSTATE PATIENT

130.

A man we know went into the hospital with an inflamed prostate and was put into a semi-private room with another man. The other looks over at him and says, stutteringly, "Wh-wh-what a-a-are y-y-you in f-f-f-for?" To which he replies that he has prostatis. The other says, "Wh-wh-what i-i-is pr-pr-pros-pros ta-ta-tatis?" To this he replies, "Well the net effect of it is that I pee like you talk."

THE BRASS RAT

131.

Now, picture, if you will, a guy who has just been stripped bare, by the lawyers, in a bloody divorce case. He is down to $5.00, so to cheer himself up, he goes into a pawn shop and asks the prop what he can get for the fiver. The prop looks around and says, "The only thing I have here for five bucks is this little brass rat, but if you buy it the sale is final and there'll be no refund." So the guy buys it and starts down the street. As he passes a third-world grocery store a rat comes out of the store and follows him; next he goes thru a warehouse district and notices an ever-growing parade of rats has joined the first one, literally on his heels, so to speak. The procession keeps being added to until the rats number in the thousands. He next crosses a bridge to get to the other side of the river, and when he gets half way he throws the brass rat into the river, and all the real live rats follow their brass brother into the water and, of course they drown. Seeing this, our hero runs back to the pawn shop and collars the owner, "You remember me; I'm the guy who bought the brass rat earlier today..." The owner says, "Now, I told you that the sale was final and no refunds..." Whereupon, the shopper says, "No, no!! I'm not looking for a refund, I just wanted to know if you have any brass lawyers."

THE REASONABLE HIT MAN

132.

Picture, if you will...a married man who has been betrayed by his wife with another man. He finds out about it and through connections locates a hit man whom he is now interviewing and briefing. The hit man has told him that he charges $25,000 a shot and never misses.

The two of them are up on a hill from which point with the high-powered Austrian scope on the hit man's rifle they can see right into the man's bedroom. They have been there for about a half an hour when their patience is rewarded. The man's wife and her lover, a large black man, have entered the room and disrobed.

The husband is incensed and tells the hit man that the contract is his. "I want you to shoot him in the cock and shoot her in the head; do it! do it! do it!, he says. Whereupon, the hit man says, "Hold on a minute; I think I can save you $25,000.00!"

THE PLIGHT OF THE SOUTH DADE TOMATO FARMERS

133.

Picture, if you will...the tomato-growing area of Miami-Dade County, down near Florida City. Harvest time is approaching. The tomatoes are big and round and firm, but they are **GREEN**. The farmers are almost in a panic because the transient pickers are ready to get to work.

So the farmers have a meeting and decide to seek help with the problem. They call in the Agricultural Extension Agent from Tallahassee who comes down to inspect the fields. After he has thus acquainted himself personally with the situation he says, "This is a very unusual problem, but not unique. The solution is a little bizarre, but effective."

The farmers react, "What do you mean by 'bizarre'?" And the agent says, "Well, it's just about full-moon time; tomorrow morning at two o'clock go out into your fields dressed in nothing but a raincoat and flash your tomatoes. I think you will find that by sunrise they will be red and ready for picking."

So they each do this and are very pleased to see that the process works; at dawn their tomatoes are not only big and round and firm, but also **RED** and ready for picking. So they call in the pickers. That is, all but a lady farmer in the vicinity who somehow had not been invited to the meeting with the man from Tallahassee. She sees that the picking is under way on the other farms, so she hustles over to a neighbor and says, "How come your tomatoes are red and being picked, while mine are big and round and firm, but **GREEN**?"

The other farmer apologizes for not having invited her to the meeting and tells her about the solution to the problem suggested by the agent. So she goes back to her farm, and the next morning she goes out at two A.M. with nothing on but a raincoat and flashes her fields, then impatiently awaits the sunrise so she can view the red ripe beauties.

So at dawn she rushes out into the fields and finds that her tomatoes are big and round and firm, but still **GREEN**. However, she notices that her cucumbers have grown four inches!

THE VIRGIN DIVORCEE

134.

A few weeks ago a young lady of about 27 came into my office to see about getting a divorce. She was quite attractive, had a very nice figure, was dressed in a basic black number, cute hat, short veil; a very nice package indeed.

She said that a friend had recommended me and that she wanted to get a divorce. I pulled out an information sheet for my file and asked her some basic questions among which was "Have you ever been married before?" She said "Yes, I have been married six times…and I'm still a virgin."

I expressed extreme surprise in view of the fact that she was so beautiful in all her aspects. I asked her to enlarge and explain, and she said, "Well, my first husband was a midget, and he wasn't up to it. My second was a private detective, and he couldn't find it. My third husband was a lawyer, and all he did was argue with it. My fourth was a photographer, and all he wanted to do was take pictures of it. My fifth was a Frenchman, and my present husband is a Greek!"

THE SELMA STORY

135.

Let me take you back to the day when the small town of Selma, Alabama, was in the news about a segregation disruption. Now, picture, if you will…a black man about to get on the Greyhound Bus with his yellow cardboard suitcase with the strap around it. As his foot hits the first step, a friend of his on the scene says, "Leroy, wheah iz you going?" Leroy answers, "Ah's leavin' town; ah done got a lettuh fum de Ku Klux Klan!" "Zat raht; whut do de lettuh say?," asks the friend. Leroy replies, "Ah doan know; ah's gonna read it on de bus!"

THE PINK MINK

136.

Picture, if you will...a very elegant fur salon in the Bal Harbour Shops. A black lady comes in and hails a sales consultant and says, "Ah'd lak to see sumpin in a fuh coat; ah's got de money raht heah to pay fo it (patting her handbag)." The rather snooty sales lady says, "Certainly, Madam, make yourself comfortable; I'll be right back."

She leaves the immediate area briefly and returns with a sort of ratty-looking fur coat, hoping to make the sale quickly and get the customer out fast. The latter looks at the coat with intense disinterest and disappointment and says: "Das not zackly whut ah had in mahnd; ah'd like sumpin a little bit niceah dan dat, sumpin mo' 'spensive!"

So the servicing person takes the coat and disappears again, to return with a full-length pink mink coat, hoping again to conclude the matter swiftly. She drapes it around the shoulders of the prospect with ill-disguised distaste and steps back. She says, "Das mo' lak whut ah had in mind; whut does dis cost?" The highly-inflated sticker price is quoted to the customer; many thousands of dollars, to which the latter replies, "Das fahn; ah think ah'll take dis: wait a minute; you doan think dis makes me look too Jewish, duz ya?"

TOTO AND GARGANTUA

137.

The St. Louis Zoo, wherein resided one of their premier attractions, namely, viz and to wit: Toto, the largest female gorilla in captivity, decided to acquire a male gorilla having in mind ultimately to be able to tell the world that they had the first baby gorilla ever born in captivity.

Their search zeroed in on the Ringling Bros.-Barnum & Bailey Circus, the proud owner of the deservedly-famous Gargantua, the largest and most ferocious-looking male in the world. They bargained successfully with the circus folks and were blessed with a great deal of publicity concerning the forthcoming acquisition and the prospective mating of the two animals.

Unfortunately, while en route to St. Louis, Gargantua mysteriously died, and, of course this put a large crimp in the St. Louis Zoo's plan. The board met and cogitated concerning damage control and alternatives, finally coming up with a plan: they would advertise for someone to mate with Toto.

The advertisement produced one sole applicant, a great huge large black fellow named Leroy. They brought him in to a conference with the members of the *ad hoc* committee handling this project which was assembled outside Toto's cage and said to him, "Now, Leroy, we are going to offer you five hundred dollars to mate with Toto." He replied, "Ah doan know; look at de fangs on dat an'mul; she'd jes chew me to death." "Now don't worry about that; we'll put a catcher's mask on her and she won't be able to bite you," they countered. "Yeah, but look at de sahz of dose hans; de'd squeeze de lahf raht outta me," said Leroy. "Now we can handle that problem; we'll but boxing gloves on her, and she won't be able to get a grip on you; and we'll give you a direct line telephone from the cage to our office, and if you have any questions, you can call us."

With these accommodations and assurances, Leroy entered the cage, and the committee went back to the office. About five minutes later the phone rang; it was the connection to the cage. Leroy said "Hello; say, how kin ah get dis catchuh's mask off; I wanta kiss the lil darlin'!"

THE MATTRESS

138.

Picture, if you will…Macy's mattress department. A large black man enters. On his back he is carrying a king-size mattress, He says, "Ah bought dis mattress heah las Tuesdy, and ah'm afraid ah've gotta return it." The sales consultant, says, "I don't know why you would be unsatisfied with that mattress; it's one of the top mattresses we sell." "Ah doan know…it might be okay fo' you whaht folks, but it feeds back a lil too fast fo' dis ole cullud boy!"

MAURICE THE MAGNIFICENT

139.

Picture, if you will…an American couple, newlyweds, on their honeymoon in Paris. After a few days of overindulging their animal instincts, they decide that they want to go out on the town, so to speak. The husband suggests that they might check out Place Pigalle; someone had told him that it was where the action was. So they proceed to that location, and the first thing they see is a marquee which says, "MAURICE THE MAGNIFICENT; SPECIAL LIMITED ENGAGEMENT." This piques their curiosity, so they enter the theater. A few minutes later the house lights dim and the curtains part. A scantily-clad young lady of beautiful composition sets up a small table about the size of a bridge table, drapes it to the floor with a black cloth and then lines up three walnuts upon it. She then retires stage left. Immediately trumpets blare a grand flourish, and Maurice The Magnificent strides out onto the stage, a handsome figure of a man dressed in a black cloak with a red satin lining. The trumpets grow silent, and Maurice whips out his hoo-hoo and whap! whap! whap! he shatters the three walnuts. The audience goes wild; this is what they came to see. The act is over.

Now, twenty-five years later the same couple is in Paris to celebrate that milestone, and after a long day of trying to do what they had done years before, they wend their way to Place Pigalle to see what is going on. They are astounded to see that the same marquee says the same thing, "Maurice the Magnificent; Special Limited Engagement." "This we gotta see," says the husband, his curiosity fully aroused. She agrees, and they enter the theater and take their seats.

The format is the same, but of course there is a different young lady. There is one difference in the set up, however, namely, instead of walnuts the girl lines up three coconuts on the table. Trumpets flourish as before, and out comes Maurice looking as handsome as ever and in the same costume. He whips out his hoo-hoo and whap! whap! whap! he destroys the three coconuts. Again the crowd goes crazy...coconuts no less!

The husband is amazed, as is his wife. He says, "We've got to go back stage and get the story on this! They manage to find the young lady who had set up the stage and tell her that they saw the act 25 years earlier and that instead of coconuts, walnuts were used. "Yes," says the girl, "Eeet is veree sad; his eyes, zey are going!"

THE BEAR HUNTER

140.

Picture, if you will...a bear hunter. He sneaks up on a great huge large bear, takes careful aim and fires. He rushes over to view the corpse, but when he arrives at the scene, he discovers no corpse at all. He feels a tap on his shoulder and turns around only to see the bear looming over him. The bear says, "You were trying to kill me, but you missed; your penalty is that you now have to give me a blow job." The hunter is mortified, but what can he do. The next day he goes out and buys a better gun with a more accurate sight, locates the same bear, sneaks up closer, takes aim and fires, with the same result. Again, the tap on the shoulder. The bear says, "You are still trying to kill me, but again you missed; you know the routine (pointing down)." So the hunter complies, totally pissed off. He vows revenge for the gross humiliation and goes out and purchases an elephant gun with a large bore and the best sight available. He locates the same bear, sneaks up to within 20 yards of him, takes careful aim and fires. He rushes forward to at last see the corpse of the object of his hatred, only, alas, to find that he has missed for a third time. Again, he feels the tap on the shoulder and turns around. The bear looks down at him and says: "Come on now, tell me the truth. You're not out here for the hunting, are you?"

THE AVANT GARDE FUNERAL HOME

141.

Picture, if you will...a funeral home. They have just brought in a new director who decides to try a new tack in promoting their services. One morning it is observed by the general public that they have erected a new sign atop their establishment which reads: LET OUR STAFF STUFF YOUR STIFF.

Down the street there exists a brothel, and the madam having seen the new sign calls in the sign painter and commissions a new sign for her establishment. The next day it is in place. It reads, LET OUR STUFF STIFF YOUR STAFF.

THE VIRGIN DIVORCEE II

142.

Picture, if you will...a lawyer's office. A rather striking lady of about 26 is there to discuss her wish to institute a divorce proceeding against her current husband. In response to some background questions posed by the attorney she reveals that this is her third marriage and she is still a virgin. The incredulous barrister inquires further asking her to please explain how this can be possible in light of the fact she is drop-dead gorgeous and all. She says, "Well, my first husband was gay, and he wouldn't do it. My second was impotent, and he couldn't do it. Now my present husband is a supply-side economist, and all he does is tell me how good it's going to be!"

THE USE OF THE FINGERS IN BUSINESS

143.

This is the story of a poor immigrant tailor whose domestic career as such starts off in a small room in the back of a tailor shop in a poor section of New York City many years ago. He is very industrious and works until late at night seven days a week. This eventually pays off in spades; he develops this humble beginning into a string of haberdashery stores sprinkled throughout upper-eastern states and is able to send his beautiful boy, Samuel, to Harvard business school. His graduation eventuates in due course, and Poppa attends the commencement exercises.

After he has the tearful pleasure to seeing his son graduate with honors, Poppa puts his arm around Sam's shoulders and says, "Samuel, my boy, I'm proud of you; you done good. As a graduation present to you I'm making you a full pahtna in da business!"

"That's very generous Poppa; I think I can help." "Tell me, Samuel, vot did dey teach you in business school dat kin be of help to da business?" "Well, they taught me tax accounting and streamlined business procedures...that sort of thing...I'm sure what I have learned will be a benefit to the chain."

"Tell me, my boy, did dey teach you da use of da fingahs in business?" "The use of the fingers, Poppa? What do you mean?" "Vell, da fingahs ah very impordant in business. Take de thumb for egzemple, dis is used for hintroductions: 'Mr. Goldberg (pointing his thumb to the left), meet Mr. Schvartz (pointing his thumb to the right)."

"De index fingah is used for pushing da kesh registah (making an appropriate gesture simulating such use of the finger in question)."

"De third fingah is used in conjunction mit de thumb to feel the de qvality of de goods (using appropriate feeling gesture involving the two digits in question.)"

"De fourth fingah is used for counting da money; alvays towards you; nevah avay from you (pointing his finger downward and moving it toward him quickly and repeatedly while speaking.)"

"What about the little finger, Poppa?" says his son. To which Poppa says, (while picking his nose with said finger), "Purely social!"

<u>I WANT TO SPEAK TO MY WIFE</u>

144.

Picture, if you will...a corporate executive in his plush office with a view. It's 10:00 A.M. He dials his home and the housemaid answers the phone. He says, "I'd like to speak to the missus." She replies, "I'm sorry, sir, but she can't come to the phone right now; she's busy." He says, "What do you mean she's busy?" The maid said, "I'm sorry, sir, but I can't tell you that." "What do you mean you can't tell me that. Listen, if you don't tell me why she can't come to the phone right now, I'm going to call Immigration and you'll be back in Guatemala by noon tomorrow; you understand?" "Yes, sir; all right, she's in bed with some man."

"Okay; now I have instructions for you. In the upper right hand drawer of my desk you'll find a loaded revolver; you get it out, leave this phone off the hook, go to the bedroom and shoot both of them, and I want to hear two shots; do you understand me?" "Yes, I understand, but I don't think I could do anything like that...". "Okay, back you go to Guatemala." "All right, sir, I'll do what you say."

About two minutes later the man hears two distinct shots, and then the maid is back on the line. "I did it, sir; they're both dead." "Okay, now I have further instructions: you go back to the bedroom and drag both the bodies out back and throw them in the river; you got that?" With this the maid says, "River? We doan have any river." To which the man says, "Isn't this 438-2571?"

<u>HOSPITALITY</u>

145.

Picture, if you will...a railroad station in a small town in Sussex, England. People are boarding the train for London. Among those thus engaged is an Episcopal minister and a man who is thanking someone who apparently has been his host for the weekend. He says, "Thanks, awfully, Reggie; it was a splendid weekend; that new chef of yours is a gem, the company was mahvelous, and your wife is one hell of a good lay I must say! They part with a handshake, and the erstwhile guest and the Episcopal minister wind up in the same compartment. Several minutes pass in silence. Finally the minister can hold back no longer and says, "Excuse me, sir, but did I hear correctly back there in the station? Did you tell that gentleman that, and I quote, "…your wife is a helluva a good lay." "Yes, as a matter of fact I did say that. Ekchually she isn't a good lay at all, but Reggie is such a swell fellow…"

THE INSULT

146.

Picture, if you will…a guy and a girl in his car; they have just arrived at a place known locally as "lovers' lane". The guy has been trying to get a date with this girl for several months, and finally through friends it has been arranged. He has taken her to a nice restaurant for a gourmet meal in the French tradition accompanied by a fine wine.

He is optimistic, so he unzips his trousers, whips out his hoo-hoo and takes and places her hand right on the member. Well! this the girl does not intend to take, so she says, "I've never been so insulted in my life! Here I've known you just a few hours, and you do this to me. And to think my friends have a high opinion of you. Boy! Have you ever got them conned! Take me home immediately, and I don't care to hear from you ever again…" And on and on, all the way back to her house she keeps up the raving and ranting.

Finally he pulls up in front of her house and says, "Okay, we're here at your house, and I've listened to your scathing harangue for the last twenty minutes, and I have just one thing to say to you: **LET GO!**

THE FRESH CHICKEN

147.

Picture, if you will…the chicken division of the meat department of a popular grocery store. A lady is speaking to the man in charge of poultry; she says, "I want a really fresh chicken. The last one I got here must have been nine years old!"

The grocer goes into the cooler and returns with a chicken which he places on the counter in front of the customer and says, "I think you will find this chicken to your liking; I can assure you that it is indeed fresh."

Whereupon, the lady examines the chicken closely; she lifts each wing and sniffs. She then spreads the legs wide, sticks her nose into the cavity, sniffing deeply and noisily. "Euuuuch!", she exclaims. "This chicken is not fresh at all!" "Come now, Madam," the grocer says, "be fair; I venture to say that even the Queen of Sheba couldn't have passed that kind of inspection."

THE ALMOND DAIQUIRI

148.

A doctor we know stops by this little bar every Friday afternoon upon leaving his office for the week end. Richard, the bartender, makes a very tasty almond daiquiri which is what the doctor always orders. One Friday afternoon the doctor walks in at the usual time, and Richard discovers that he is all out of almonds, so he whips up the drink using another kind of nut. The doctor takes one sip and says, "This is not an almond daiquiri, Dick!" To which the bartender says, "No, that's a hickory daiquiri, Doc!"

THE KOALA

149.

Picture, if you will…an upscale singles cocktail lounge in a major hotel. A koala comes in, hops up onto a stool and orders a drink. A really striking-looking girl at the other end of the bar gets up, comes over and sits next to him. She says, "Boy! Are you ever CUTE! What are you?" The koala says, "I'm a koala, and I'm not only cute, but I am cuddly, and I give the best head in the world!" "She says, "Well, I'm a pro, and I know all about head, but I've never had a koala, so let's go up to my room; I'm right here in the hotel."

So they go up to her room, and the koala gives a demonstration of his talent as a head man. Then about two hours later after the girl has experienced major and multiple orgasms, the koala gets up and starts to get dressed. She says, "Where are you going?" And he replies, "I'm outta here." To which she responds, "Just a minute; aren't you forgetting something; before we came up here I told you I was a professional, which as you know, is a euphemism for a call girl. Let me show you what Webster's says about the word 'prostitute'. Here it is, 'Prostitute: a woman who makes love for money.'"

"Okay," says the koala, "I'll go along with the dictionary bit; let's see what it says about Koala; here it is: 'Koala: A cute and cuddly little furry creature indigenous to Australia that eats bushes and **LEAVES'**; I'm outta here."

THE MERGER

150.

There was an item in the Wall Street Journal the other day that caught my eye. It said that there was a mega merger in the works involving four well-known and highly respected corporate entities, The Yale Lock Company, a familiar name to all; Mary Tyler Moore Enterprises, the entertainment conglomerate; Fuller Brush Company, a name we all know, and W.R. Grace & Company, the huge shipping concern. The emerging entity will be known as Yale, Mary, Fuller Grace!!

SUBJECT CROSS-INDEX
References are to joke numbers

G.

H.

I.

ITALIANS/ITALY, 61, 70

J.

JESUS, 35
JEWISH, 20, 143
JOB, 45, 66
JUMPING, 92

K.

KILTS, 100
KNIFE, 105

L.

LANGUAGE/LINGUISTICS, 22, 23
LEGS, 70, 81
LETTUCE, 6
LYNCHING, 15

M.

MARRIAGE, 4, 95, 117, 134, 142
MEAT, 57, 98
MEN, 71, 89
MERCEDES, 78
MEXICO, 8
MOTHER, 128
MOTHER SUPERIOR, 3, 18, 61
MOUTH-TO-MOUTH, 49

N.

NATIVES, 39, 65
NATIVE AMERICANS, 62, 120
NAVY, 63, 75, 87
NOVITIATE, 3, 115
NUNS, 3, 18, 19, 61, 115

O.

OBSCENITIES, 103, 108
OFFICES, 45
OLD FOLKS/OLD FOLKS' HOMES, 24, 32, 80
OPERATIONS, 13
ORGASM, 9

P.

Q.

R.

S.

Picture,
If You Will...

VOLUME CHOO

By Richard R. Booth

MORE MATERIAL FOR THE EMERGING HUMORIST

ISBN: 0-7596-9028-6 (ebook)
ISBN: 0-7596-9029-4 (softcover)

This book is printed on acid free paper.

1stBooks – rev. 04/26/02

<u>TABLE OF CONTENTS</u>
References Are To Joke Numbers

BEST CHILI IN TOWN

1.

Picture, if you will...a diner-type eating establishment. A gent comes in, sits down and orders a bowl of chili. He came in specifically to get a bowl of chili...this place is noted for its chili. The counter chap says, "I'm sorry, sir, but I just gave the gentleman on your right the last bowl we had."

Our guy looks over to his right. The man is reading a newspaper. A full bowl of chili is sitting there on the counter in front of him, so he says to the latter, "I notice that you're not eating that bowl of chili, and if you don't want it, I'd like it; the chili here is the best in town." Whereupon, the other says, "Be my guest."

At this, our friend drags the bowl over in front of him and starts eating...savoring each spoonful practically in a state of ecstasy. Well, about four spoonfuls into the process he sees a dead mouse in the chili and promptly throws up right into the bowl, and can you blame him?

Seeing this, the other says, "That's about as far as I got, too!"

SKYDIVING RELUCTANCE

2.

Did you know that there has been only one blind skydiver in the relatively short history of the sport. He quit after just three jumps? It scared the s—t out of his dog!

THE EYES HAVE IT

3.

Picture, if you will...an eye doctor's office; the doctor is examining the bloodshot eyes of a new patient. He says, "Hmmmm! Yes, I can tell you what your problem is: You have herpes of the eyes; you've been looking for love in all the wrong places."

NATIONALITY ESTABLISHED

4.

Current research has established that it is quite likely that Adam (of Garden of Eden fame) was Polish. They explain it as follows: "In the Garden of Eden there was Eve and there was an apple; and Adam ate the apple."

THE CORONATION

5.

There is a small country in Africa whose government is patterned closely after that of Great Britain. Their parliament has been established, and it has been determined that they would also have a monarchy. To this end, the government sends an envoy to London to search through the archives for a detailed description of the coronation of Queen Elizabeth II. The archival search bears fruit, and the envoy returns with a certified transcript of the actual ceremony.

In due course a queen is selected, and the the coronation is scheduled. Parliament deems it appropriate to invite the various world governments to the ceremony and is extremely excited when the British government advises that a personal envoy from the Queen will be in attendance. In fact the person who is thusly delegated to represent Britain had actually witnessed Queen Elizabeth's coronation and volunteers to assist in the planning of the ceremony. He is enthusiastically welcomed, and they eagerly accept his offer to help with the planning and staging.

When the envoy arrives they schedule a "dress rehearsal", so to speak, so as to elicit the comments of their visitor from London. The ceremony is necessarily different in one respect, since the young ladies in this emerging nation always go topless, but other than that, they have vowed to follow the original scenario devotedly.

They establish a long aisle down which the coronation party is to proceed to the altar area where the crown is to be placed on the queen's head, and lining this aisle on each side are fifty of the comeliest young women in the country that are proudly thrusting their naked charms forward.

The rehearsal guests take their places, the girls lining up on either side, and the sounds of low conversations permeate the hall. At this point a young man runs down one side of the aisle and up the other deftly touching the nipples of each of the topless young ladies with the palm of his hand as he passes.

Well, the British envoy, who is helping with the planning is almost shocked; he takes aside the protocol official from the host country that is in charge of the ceremony and says, "You told me that you were going to faithfully follow the script of the ceremony that took place when our beloved Queen was crowned, and I think you will admit that nowhere in the transcript is there any mention of what I just observed; I'm quite sure of that!"

"But," said the man in charge, "I *am* following the script with which I was provided by your archives. Look here it is, right here…" (pointing to the document), and the other looked, and there it was in parentheses, "(At this point a titter ran through the crowd.)"

THE ENGAGEMENT

6.

Picture, if you will…a five-year-old boy named Johnny talking to the father of his friend, Mary, also 5 years old, "Mr. Johnson, I love Mary, and she loves me, and so we want to get married. I was told by my father that I had to speak to you first."

Mary's father thinks that is mighty cute, so he decides to play it straight with the little boy. "Well, Johnny", I think you're a neat little kid, and I'm sure that you and Mary love each other, but when you get married you have to assume certain responsibilities; for example you'll have to support Mary as you wife."

"Yes, I know," says Johnny, proudly, "I'm going to be helping my big brother with his paper route."

"Well, that's fine," says old dad, "but if you and Mary get married, you are liable to have a baby, and that is an added responsibility!"

"Yes, I know; Mary and I have talked about that, and we have decided that if Mary lays an egg, I'm going to step on it!!"

A LOCAL PROBLEM

7.

The scene is the Dade County Courthouse; there is a great, huge, large plethora of buzzards soaring above and around its pyramidal peak. It's a seasonal problem; in the Summer they go to Ohio, and they return to Miami when the tourists start trickling down to South Florida. The core of the problem is that they are messy and numerous, so the County Commission authorizes search ads to be placed in some of the big-city dailies, countrywide.

The ad campaign bears fruit when a man from the North comes in to a commission meeting with a proposal: for $20,000 he will undertake to rid the area of the buzzard problem; further, he will guarantee to do this within one week, in default of which he will pay the county $10,000. The commission is greatly impressed by his confidence and willingness to put up $10,000 if he fails, so they accept his win-win proposal, and the respective sums are placed in escrow to await the outcome.

The following day the entrepreneur appears on the ground floor terrace with a pink buzzard on his forearm, like a falcon, sort of. Up above the buzzards are soaring, whirling and diving. The proponent then swings his business arm upward in a swift arc, and the pink buzzard streaks for that part of the heavens just above the courthouse. It gets into the swing of the regular buzzard routine with the native group, swirling around, and after about five minutes it takes off to the East. Strangely enough all the buzzards follow the lead of old pinky, just like the Pied Piper of Hameln, so to speak. Everyone sweats out the stipulated week and the buzzards are never seen again. The problem has been solved! The commission and others rejoice unto the Heavens.

So, the hero picks up the escrow, and starts to leave; whereupon, Commissioner O'Reilly takes him aside and says to him, "You wouldn't happen to have a pink Cuban, would you?"

THE PROSPECTIVE DEPOSITOR

8.

Picture, if you will…a bank lobby; a man is standing before a teller's window; he says, "I think I'd like to open a f—in' bank account…maybe look at a couple of f—in' CD's."

The teller, a lady who has been with the bank for many years, is terribly offended by the language that is coming from the man who seems to be interested in becoming a depositor, and she says, "I don't appreciate your language, mister, and unless you clean up your language and be more respectful, discreet and polite I won't deal with you and you can leave the premises."

"You don't have to get so excited, lady, all I said was that I am thinking of depositing my money in your f—in' bank."

Well, this causes a bit of a row, and the manager of the bank becomes aware that something is going on that merits his attention, so he goes to the teller's cage and asks what the noise is all about.

The teller, practically in tears, says, "This man is using the most horrible language, and I don't think I should have to put up with it!"

At this point, the man says, "I don't know what the fuss is; I just won the f—in' lottery, and I want to open a f—in' bank account."

With this, the bank manager grabs him by the elbow and leads him away, saying, "I'm sorry that c—t gave you such a hard time, sir; just come this way and we'll take care of the details."

THE INVESTIGATOR'S REPORT

9.

Picture, if you will…the office of a private detective who has been hired to investigate the activities of a man's wife who is suspected of having an affair. The husband wants to get proof of the illicit affair before he files for divorce.

The P.I. is reading his report to the suspicious husband, "At 9:00 P.M. on Tuesday, the 27th, I placed subject wife under surveillance in her home. I was situated in a tree outside her bedroom and had an unobstructed view. She was dressed in a lacy black negligee and was lying on the bed alone. At 9:17 P.M. on said date, I observed from said post a man entering the house. She left the bedroom to greet the man, and the two of them returned to the bedroom. She removed the man's jacket, shirt, tie, trousers, shoes and socks leaving him in a pair of white Fruit-of-the-Loom briefs. They lay down on the bed and kissed and fondled each other at length. At this point, precisely at 9:42 P.M., the subject leaned over and switched off the light. At 11:00 P.M. on said night I observed said man leaving the house, entering a car and driving off. I ended the surveillance at this point."

"See," said the husband, "there's always that doubt!"

THE NEWLYWED'S LAMENT

10.

Picture, if you will...a newlywed young JAP; she was married less than six months ago. She has come home to Momma complaining bitterly that she just can't live with her husband another single day, her lament being that practically every other word he uses is a four-letter word.

Momma says, "You can't be that naïve, darling, why whenever you go to the movies they use four-letter words all the time. The same with cable t-v. Let's face it, it's part of life whether you like it or not. Just what does he say that upsets you so much?"

"I can't tell you, Momma; I just can't bring myself to say those words! she says. "Oh, come, come now, dear; you can tell me; I'm your mother. Tell me what are the words that he says that offend you so?" To which the daughter says, "They're terrible: Cook, bake, wash, iron...!"

GOD'S VACATION

11.

St. Peter and God are having a conversation concerning God's vacation plans. He suggests to the latter that perhaps he might like to go to Mercury. God rejects that idea saying the Mercury is too bloody hot. Next, St. Peter suggests Pluto, and that is rejected as "too bloody cold." Then St. Peter says that perhaps He might want to go to Earth, not too hot, not too cold.

"Nah," says God, "The last time I was there 2000 years ago I knocked up a young Jewish girl, and I've been hearing about that ever since!"

KEEP THE STATUS QUO

12.

Picture, if you will...a nice New York Jewish American Princess, who through exceptionally good luck winds up married to a very wealthy Greek shipping magnate who whisks her off to his country in his private 747 where she lives a life of sheer luxury. He also is very generous with her parents to whom he gives a new stretch limo with a pre-paid chauffeur, country club memberships, couturier clothing, all kinds of expensive presents.

Six months pass, and she appears in New York on her parents' door step, virtually in tears. Her father says, "Vot's diss?" She says, "I can't stand it any more, I'm leaving him." Her father says, "Vot kent you stand?" The girl replies, "It's the sex; I can't stand the sex!" "Vot's wrong mit de sex you kent stand?"

She says, "When I left New York my anus was the size of a dime, and now it's the size of a silver dollar!"

To this her father says, "You mean you want to make all this trouble over 90 cents?!!"

AT THE RESTAURANT

13.

Picture, if you will…a couple from the midwest in New York for a week to see some shows and check out some great restaurants. A gourmet friend from back home says that there is a restaurant in New York that is better than any restaurant he has ever eaten anyplace, but, he says, "There is one thing wrong with the operation; they don't take reservations, so if you want the experience you'll have to go there and wait."

Well, this intrigues them, and they decide to try and get in, so they go to the address in question and just manage to get inside the front door. The place is packed with people who are milling about the entrance to the dining room, and all of them are masturbating like crazy.

They have never seen such mass social depravity in their lives, and they wonder why their friend back home didn't tell them about this sort of scene, so they get the attention of the maitre d' and ask him to please explain what is taking place.

The maitre d' is quick to explain that the demand for dining in this establishment is so great because of its gourmet reputation that they had to institute this new system: "First come, first served."

THE APPROPRIATE REMEDY

14.

Picture, if you will…a small town pharmacy; a young man has applied for employment there, and the owner/pharmacist tells him that he will give him a try and if it develops that he has an aptitude for this sort of work, then he will consider hiring him to work there full time.

So, the boy don's the white jacket that is the accepted uniform for employees in small town pharmacies and goes to work. Right off a gentleman comes in and, approaching him, says that he needs something for a nagging cough that he has had for several days. The young man, says, "I have just the thing for that; it should be very effective." Whereupon he sells the man a package of EX-LAX, tells him to take the whole package and eat it like a candy bar, and the man leaves.

The pharmacist observes what in his view is an outrageously inappropriate sale, collars the applicant/employee and says, "Why on earth would you sell a man with a nagging cough a package of EX-LAX? It doesn't make sense; don't you know that EX-LAX is a powerful laxative, not a cough remedy?"

At this, the boy takes the owner over to the front door of the store and points to the customer leaning against a tree across the street in the town square. "Look," he says, "He's not coughing like he was when he came in; I think the EX-LAX cured him; he doesn't dare cough!"

ON THE DEATH BED

15.

Picture, if you will...a man on his death bed; the doctor has told everyone that he could die any minute. His wife is sitting there patiently waiting for the final moments. Feeling remorse over sins he has committed he tells his wife, "Darling, I can die any minute now; there are things on my conscience that I must tell you so I can go more peacefully. I wanted to tell you that I had had intercourse with both your sister and your mother."

"Yes, I know;" she says, "That's why I poisoned you!"

THE GOLFER AND WIFE #2

16.

Picture, if you will...an avid golfer with all the best equipment. He is playing with his wife. On the fourth hole his drive slices badly and winds up behind a barn; he does not have a clear shot to the green. His wife surveys the situation and says, "Dear, look; the barn door is open, and so is the door at the other end. If you look through the barn I think you can see the green. I think that if you play through the barn you have an off chance of hitting the green." Her husband checks out what she says and sees that she is right, so he takes his five wood and gives it a mighty swipe. Well the ball hits the side of the barn and bounces back striking his wife in the head, killing her instantly. He is devastated, but life must go on.

After a suitable mourning period, the golfer takes unto himself a new wife who is also a golfer. One Saturday he is playing the same course and on the fourth hole gets into the same predicament as before. His new wife says, "Look dear, if you sight through the open doors of the barn I think you might be able to put it right on the green."

To this the husband says, "I don't think I'll try that. Last year I found myself in this same position, and I tried hitting through the barn as you suggest, and it was a big mistake; I would up with a double bogey.

WHAT DO YOU CALL...?

17.

What do you call a mushroom with a nine-inch stem?
Answer: A fun guy to be with.

THE SPELLING EXERCISE

18.

Picture, if you will...a classroom. Teach says, "I'm going to give you some words. You spell them and use them in a sentence, okay?"

She calls on Shandra Jo and says, "Dumb." The girl says, "D-u-m-b, Leroy is dumb." Then teach gives her the word "stupid". Shandra Jo says, "S-t-u-p-i-d; Leroy is stupid."

Then the teacher calls on Leroy and says, "Dictates." And Leroy says, "Shandra Jo says my dictates good."

MORE USAGE

19.

Teacher says to one of her high school students, "Jasbo, use the word 'fascinates' in a sentence.

He says, "Mona has a blouse on today that has ten buttons, but her tits are so big she can only fascinate."

THE NEW PET

20.

A man we know is bereaved; his dog which had been a part of his household for many years dies, and he buries it. He goes to the pub and has a few pints to assuage his grief, and while he is there he buys a monkey to replace the dog. He takes the monkey home and tells his wife that he bought the monkey to take the place of the dog. She says, "Where is the monkey going to sleep?" and her husband says, "He's going to sleep in the bed with us, of course." And she says, What about the smell?" And he replies, "I got used to it, so can he."

ANOTHER PET

21.

What do you do if a pit bull humps your leg?
Answer: You fake an orgasm."

YOU KNOW IT'S GOING TO BE A DISMAL DAY, IF...

22.
   1. You wake up face down on the sidewalk.
   2. You phone SUICIDE PREVENTION and they put you on HOLD.
   3. Your birthday cake collapses from the weight of the candles.
   4. You turn on the TV news, and they're showing the emergency routes out of the city.
   5. You wake up and discover that your waterbed broke and then realize that you don't have a waterbed.
   6. Your wife wakes up feeling amorous and you have a headache.
   7. Your horn goes off accidentally and remains stuck as you follow a group of Hell's Angels down the freeway.
   8. Your boss tells you not to bother to take off your coat.
   9. The bird singing outside your window is a buzzard.

10. You call your answering service, and they tell you it's none of your business.
11. Your blind date turns out to be your ex-wife.
12. The check with which you paid your income tax bounces.
13. Your pet rock snaps at you.
14. Your wife says, "Good morning, Bill" and your name is George.
15. (If you're a chick) You put on your bra backwards, and it fits better.
16. (Likewise) You walk to work and find that your dress is stuck in the back of your pantyhose.

DIFFERENCE BETWEEN

23.

Q. What's the difference between "kinky" and "perverted"?

A. If you use chicken feathers when you make love to your lady, that's kinky. If you use the whole chicken, that's perverted.

A MEMORABLE EVENT

24.

Picture, if you will...a cocktail lounge which is a popular place for singles to meet. A very nice-looking, clean-cut guy is seated at the bar sipping a very dry martini. He is in town on a business trip and has just concluded what he came to the city for. On the two next bar stools are Siamese twins likewise drinking martinis. He strikes up a conversation with that part of the duo sitting next to him, and one thing leads to another; finally they walk out of the bar together and go to his hotel room where they make seemingly endless love. It is very difficult to describe just what took place and between whom. Anyhow, he calls them a cab at about 3:00 A.M., and they leave.

Three months later, he is back in the city on business and, as before, he stops in the same bar to unwind with one of their very satisfactory martinis. Five minutes after starting to sip the same, he glances to his right, and catches the Siamese darlings in the act of sliding onto the next two stools. Four of the six eyes meet, and the girl says, "Remember me?"

THE WINNER

25.

Picture, if you will...a cocktail lounge which seems to attract single folks. Seated at the bar is a very handsome young man. He becomes aware of a couple sitting in one of the booths along the wall behind him. He says, under his breath, to himself, "Wow!" He has just seen the most perfectly beautiful girl ever created and immediately wants her. He calls over the bartender and says, "I'd like to meet that girl over there in that booth, the blonde with the green eyes; can you arrange that, for a fiver, maybe?"

The bartender says, "Save your money, and don't waste your time; that girl is engaged to that guy; they are getting married next month; they are totally involved with each other and have been for well over a year."

The guy says, "I think I can take her away from him; in fact I'll bet you my tab and another twenty that I can walk out of here with her within five minutes."

The bartender accepts the bet, they both put their twenties on the bar, and he goes over to the booth and sits down with the couple. Four minutes and seven seconds later he and the girl get up and head for the door, the guy scooping up the two twenties as he passes by.

The bartender can't believe that this happened, so he goes over to the booth where the girl's fiancé is still seated with a blank look on his face and asks, "What the hell happened here anyway? What did he say to her that made her desert you like that and take off with him?"

The boy friend, still virtually in shock, replies, "That's just it…he didn't say a word…he just sat there licking his eyebrows!"

IMMEDIATE REACTION

26.

Picture, if you will…a nunnery. A young pleasant-looking novitiate comes running into the office of the Mother Superior visibly upset. And well she should be upset; she has just been raped. She asks the M.S. what she should do?

The Mother Superior, very well collected, says, "You go right down to the kitchen and get a lemon out of the fridge, cut it in half, and suck out all the juice you can…do it NOW!"

The trembling girl says, "Will that keep me from getting pregnant, Mother Superior?"

"No," she replies, "but it might get that silly grin off your face.

THE WORLD'S THINNEST BOOKS

27.

Beauty Secrets, by Janet Reno.
The Thrill of Downhill Skiing, by Sonny Bono
Flying at night, by JFK, Jr.
Home-Built Airplanes, by John Denver
Things I love About Bill, by Hillary Clinton
Things I can't afford, by Bill Gates
My Plan To Find the Real Killers, by O.J. Simpson
Things I would Not Do For Money, by Dennis Rodman
My Wild Years, by Al Gore
Italian War Heroes
Navigating the Pacific by Air, by Amelia Earhart
American's Most Popular Lawyers

Detroit – A Travel Guide
Dr. Kevorkian's Collection of Motivational Speeches
Everything Men Know About Women
George Foreman's Big Book of Baby Names
Mike Tyson's Guide to Dating Etiquette
Spotted Owl Recipes, by EPA
The Comprehensive Amish Phone Directory
My Book of Family Values, by Bill Clinton

MARRIED SEX

28.

Picture, if you will...a married couple in bed in a coupled position. Man says, "Oh, I'm sorry, dear, did I hurt you?"
W. "No, why do you ask?"
M. "You moved!"

SINGLE LADY, TRAVELING ALONE

29.

Picture, if you will...a little ole lady talking to someone behind the counter in a travel agency: "Tell me, can you suggest where I might go for a vacation? I'm a single woman traveling alone."
The counter man happens to be Irish, and replies, "Well, now, Madam, hev ya ever considered goin' ta Ireland?"
"Of course not," she retorts, "it's cold and it's damp, and it's full of Catholics!"
"Well, then," he says,"Ya might wanta go ta Hell; it's hot and it's dry, and it's fulla Protestants!"

NOUVELLE DINING SPOT

30.

Two guys are talking. One says, "I hear you went to dinner at that new place that just opened; how was it?"
"Well," says the other, "If the soup had of been as warm as the wine, the wine as old as the turkey, and the chicken had breasts like the waitress, it would have been a pretty good meal!"

NICE DAY?

31.

Picture, if you will...a woman speaking to her recently acquired parrot; the parrot tends toward using salty language, and she is trying to render the parrot more genteel, so to speak. She says, to the parrot, "Nice day, isn't it?"
The parrot replies, a beautiful f—in day!"

She tries the same question again with the same result, so she grabs the parrot by the neck and swings it around her head about ten times, sets the parrot down on its perch and says, "I said, it's a nice day, isn't it?"

To this the parrot, still a bit groggy from the experience, replies, "Nice day, hell! Where were you when the f—in tornado hit?"

AT THE NUDIST COLONY

32.

A new man has arrived, he sees a rather comely young lady in her nubile buff and goes over to make her acquaintance, so to speak. He holds out his hand and says, "My name is Jim; I'm pleased to meet you, Miss."

She replies coyly, "I can see that you are!"

THE COLUMNIST'S VISIT

33.

Dave Barry, the famous Miami humorous columnist has just arrived non-stop from the West Coast where he spent ten days in a nudist colony gathering material for a column or two. His good friend Carl Hiaasin meets him at the gate and says, "Hey, Buddy, tell me, what impressed you most about your stay in the nudist colony?

To which he replies, "Cane-bottomed chairs!"

WAIT

34.

Sign on veterinarian's door:
Be Back Soon. Stay. Sit.

RELATIVE HOLINESS

35.

Picture, if you will…the Pearly Gates; Mother Teresa has just arrived and has been presented with a very nice halo and a comfortable cloud. She's there a few days and notices Princess Di floating by on a substantially similar cloud, but Di has a materially larger halo, and Mother T. is upset and complains to the management about the disparity in haloes while suggesting that her service on Earth when compared to that of Princess Di merited a larger halo than the Princess. Whereupon, she was advised by St. Peter, "Mother Teresa, we hear you, and what you say is perfectly legitimate, but if you will look closer you will see that that is not a halo on Princess Di, but a steering wheel from a Mercedes!"

THE CONFESSIONAL

36.

Picture, if you will...a Monday evening meeting in the sacristy of St. Arnold's Catholic Church between Father Reilly, the Priest and Sean Finnegan, the Deacon (who is charged with accounting for the donations collected at the various services the previous day.) Father Reilly says, "Deacon Finnegan, I note that the amount that you are turning in is way down from last week's take and the week before that and in fact is lower than any week I can recall; is it that you have been skimming a bit?" "No, Father; I haven't been skimming; the amount is a true one."

The priest then says, "Let's move over here to the confessional; I'll ask you again, and what you tell me will be in confidence." So they go over there; the priest is in the box and says, "Deacon Finnegan, tell me now; have you skimmed a sum off the top of the collection?"

To this the deacon says, "I'm sorry, Father, but I can't hear a word you are saying; there must be something wrong with the acoustics of this box." With this the priest says, "There's nothing wrong with the acoustics here; let's swap positions; you get here in the box, and we'll pursue this inquiry." So they change places, and Finnegan says, "Father Reilly, is it true that you have been seducing the little boys in the choir, like I have heard?" The priest responds, "Say, you're right, Deacon, you can't hear a word from this side!"

WHO WANTS TO BE A MILLIONAIRE?

37.

Picture, if you will...a guy and his squeeze are lying on the bed watching the latest T-V craze, "Who Wants to Be a Millionaire?" The guy is a little horny and makes a pass at the girl who is concentrating on Regis and his contestant who is trying to answer the latest question worth $32,000. She rebuffs his advance, so he says, "I think at this point, Regis, I want to call a friend!"

THE REFUGEES

38.

Picture, if you will...a rickety sailing vessel full of Cubans in the Florida straights heading for the South Florida shores and asylum. One old gentleman is quite ill and fears that he is dying and will never make it to the USA. He says, "I know I am going; I'm a good Cuban, and I want to kiss the Cuban flag before I die; someone has a Cuban flag on this boat?" All are questioned and no one has a Cuban flag on board, but a very nubile young female brunette member of the group says, "I have a Cuban flag tattooed on my ass, if that will do for you."

"Yes, my dear, that will do nicely, and thank you", he says. With this, she takes off her pants, and he proceeds to kiss her flag. When he has satisfied this wish he says, "Would you mind if you would turn over, I want to kiss Fidel goodbye, too!

THE JADED ONE

39.

Picture, if you will…a patron of this very high class bordello conversing with the Madam; he has just arrived on the premises and says to her, "Madam; I've been coming here for several years; I love your girls, but I'm really jaded; tonight I want something I've never had before."

She replies, "I've got just what you want. This is your lucky night! I have a new girl named Lola; she's up in Room 2B; she'll fulfill your wish!"

So he goes up to 2B to Lola who greets him cordially and proceeds to show him something new. It seems that she has a glass eye; she takes it out, plugs his hoo-hoo into the socket and proceeds to wink him off. He goes crazy; he's never had anything that remotely touches this for sheer sexual sensation.

After he has regained a modicum of composure, he says, "Man! That was fantastic; I want to come see you again real soon, but tomorrow I have to go to Atlanta on business; when I get back I'll call for you."

She says, "I'm glad I was able to please you tonight; have a good trip; hurry back; I'll keep an eye out for you!"

TOO MUCH OF A GOOD THING

40.

Picture, if you will…a man talking to the doctor; he is a new patient and has filled out the usual forms. The doctor is perusing what he has written and notes that the man is complaining that he has a twenty-inch hoo-hoo and no girl wants to get sexually involved with him fearing that she will be damaged by this outsized member.

The doctor verifies the complaint by examining the appendage and says, "There is nothing I can do for you, I'm afraid; surgical science has not advanced to the point where I could truncate this instrument of yours, but I know a gypsy lady over on the other side of town who can maybe direct you to someone who can give you the desired relief."

The man locates the gypsy woman in question who says, "This is not something I can personally handle, but two miles out of town to the South is a swampy area which is the habitat of a frog of my acquaintance who has mystical powers; I think he is the answer to your problem. You find the frog and say to him, 'Kiss me', and he will say 'No!' and your hoo-hoo will thereupon shrink by four inches."

The man wends his way to the swampy area in question and locates the frog, and says, "Kiss me." and the frog says, "No!" and immediately his member shrinks four inches. Now he's getting someplace, but he still has sixteen inches, which is still too big. So he again says to the frog, "Kiss me!" And the frog replies, "No! no! no! no!!!"

THE LAST WORD TO THE FIRST TWO

41.

Picture, if you will...the Garden of Eden; God is talking to Adam and Eve. He says, "Well, now, I've just about completed my creation project, but I do have two more items left in my bag of tricks for you two. The first is the ability to pee standing up; now which of you wants that?"

Adam jumps right in and says, "That's for me; I want that; you don't mind, do you Eve? I really would like to have that ability; oh yes, then I could go anywhere...behind the tree...anyplace; yes I'd like that one please, God!"

Eve isn't really excited about that particular concept, so she says, "Okay, Adam; I could care less if God were to give you that ability."

So God says, "So be it. Adam, that is yours. Now let's see what this last one is, which of course goes to Eve. Ah! Here it is: 'Multiple orgasms.'"

THE TWO MAIN POLISH LIES

42.

1.   The check is in my mouth.
2.   I won't come in your mailbox.

THE BLONDE'S CAR TROUBLE

43.

Picture, if you will...a good-looking blonde driving down a busy highway. The car conks out right in the middle of one of the lanes; whereupon, two nude men in raincoats get out of the back seat and proceed to flash all the cars in both directions: whish, whish, whish. The net effect is, of course a gigantic traffic tie up.

Finally a motorcycle cop makes his way to the scene and says to the blonde in question, "I can't believe this! What do you think you are doing here, young lady?" To which she says, "Well, officer, my car just stopped cold, so like I learned in driving class I put on my flashers!"

RELIGIOUS DIFFERENCES

44.

Picture, if you will...an ecumenical old folks home. Two couples are conversing; one is Catholic, and the other is Jewish; both couples have been married for many years. They are discussing what it is like living in a place like this, when the Catholic wife asks the Jewish couple what they like to do in the evening.

The Jewish lady says, "Vell, ve've bin marrid many years and are very close; vat ve do in de evenings is to hold hands, vatch T-V and sing old Catholic songs. Vat do you do, dollink?

In answer, the Catholic gentleman says, "Well, we've also been married for many years, and, like, you, we are very close; each other is all we have. Also like you we like to hold hands and watch our favorite T-V shows, but, unlike you, we don't know any old Jewish songs, so we f—k!

THE AMATEUR SLEUTH

45.

Picture, if you will…two ladies, good friends, in the ladies' locker room of the Country Club. They have just completed nine holes of golf and are disrobing to shower. One says to the other, "Emily, I know you have been having an affair." Emily is flabbergasted; she thought that she had fooled all her friends. "And, Emily," she says, "I know who your lover is; he's a Gypsy." Emily is completely boggled by what her friend has said. "How did you find out? I've been very discreet," says Emily. "Well," replies the other, "the tip-off is the green spots on the inside of your thighs; the rest I deduced, Emily; I concluded that he is a Gypsy, because he wears earrings, and, Emily, his earrings are not gold!"

EDUCATING JUNIOR

46.

Picture, if you will…a typical middle-class suburban household; the 13-year-old son just come home from school. His mother says, "What did you do at school today, Dear?"

Her son replies, "Same old, same old, Mom, except for the fact that I had sex with my teacher!" The magnitudinousity of this tutorial transgression completely unhinges his mother, who says, "You go up to your room and shut the door, and when your father comes home he'll really lay it on you; you can depend on that!"

In due course the father arrives from the office and is greeted by a conspicuously upset wife who blurts out what she has learned from their young son about his having had sex with his teacher. She tells him to go up to the boy's room and show him what real discipline is, so the father goes up there, goes into the room and shuts the door. The boy is really apprehensive about what is going to happen to him, virtually cowering in the corner.

The father says, "Son, your mother is really upset at what you said about having sex with your teacher, and I'm not surprised; most women would have the same reaction, I'm sure. But women don't really know about things like this. As far as I am concerned, this is a right of passages, so to speak, today you came of age, and I have to do something significant about this, so you'll remember the day. You know that red bike I had planned to give you for your birthday next month? Well, we're going right down to The Bike Shop and get it for you today!"

So they go down to the shop in question, and Dad makes the purchase, saying to his son, "Billy, you ride the bike home; I'll follow you in the car. To this Billy says, "Dad I don't think I can do that; my ass is still sore from the sex."

IS HE BACK?

47.

Father O'Reilly, whose parish has been a small community in Ireland for several years, decides he needs a vacation, so he hops a plane out of Shannon for Las Vegas to get a taste of life in America. He is no more than barely in the terminal when someone runs up to him and says, "Elvis, that's you; you're back. I knew you weren't dead!" To which he replies, "Get outta me face; I'm not Elvis; I don't look a bit like him!" Father O'Reilly then hops into a cab and says, "Take me to The Sands Hotel, and step on it." The cabby says, "Sure thing, sir...Omigod! It's Elvis; I knew you weren't dead; I'm your number one fan; it's great to see you!" "Shut up, you imbecile; I'm not Elvis! Now turn around and drive, man," says the priest. Well, the father arrives at the hotel and proceeds to the check-in counter. "Omigod! Omigod! It's you!" screams the hotel clerk, "You're back Elvis; I knew this day would come. We've got everything just the way you like it: the Elvis Suite is comped; everything for you is free; the cheeseburgers, fried peanut butter and banana sandwiches, masseuses, hookers, a full liquor bar and choice pharmaceuticals! We're so glad you're back!" Father O'Reilly looks at the hotel clerk and says, "Thank you; thank you very much!"

ANOTHER WHAT D'YA GET

48.

What d'ya get when you cross a dinosaur with a homosexual?   A Megadinosauranus.

A DOMESTIC PROBLEM

49.

Two guys are out drinking one night when one says to the Other, "Ya know, I've got a real problem; it almost interferes with my drinking. Whenever I go home after we've been drinking, I try very carefully to avoid waking up my wife. I turn off the headlights before I reach the driveway, I cut off the engine and coast into the garage. I take off my shoes before I enter the house; I sneak up the stairs and get undressed in the bathroom; I ease into bed, and my wife *still* wakes up and yells at me for staying out so late." "Well," says the other, "obviously you're using the wrong approach. I screech into the driveway, slam the door, storm up the steps, throw my shoes into the closet, jump into bed, rub my hands on my wife's butt and say, 'How about a blowjob?' And she's always sound asleep!"

DIFFERENCES

50.

What's the difference between love, true love and showing off? Spitting, swallowing and gargling.

A MINK COAT

51.

A lady sweeps into the club sporting a full-length mink coat. A girl friend says, "Wow! Did you get that after a night of great sex?" "Yes." she replies, "the one I found out about!"

THE DOGS

52.

Picture, if you will…a small-town Labor Day picnic. Right in the middle of everything these two dogs get hung up in the usual way, and several of the guys try to get them apart, but in vain. Just about when frustration is peaking a teenaged boy approaches the tableau, sticks his finger in his mouth to make it slippery, and then he forcefully shoves it up the rectal aperture of the dominant canine. Well, the result is massive and immediate. The dog who receives the thrust of the aggressive digit howls and wails, tears himself loose and flees the scene with great rapidity. One of the men in the group that had vainly tried to disentangle the animals, says to the lad, "Son, you showed some real creativity there; I've never seen that type of situation handled so successfully before. How'd you think of it?" "Well," says the lad, "that's my dog. I know him real well; he can dish it out but he can't take it!"

THE ENCHANTED FROG

53.

Picture, if you will…a stunning young lady out for a fast aerobic walk. Her route takes her by the pond in the park. As she is passing a clump of pussy willows she hears a faint voice, "Help me. Help me!" She looks around and finally determines that the plea is coming from a big bull frog on the edge of the swamp. She picks up the frog, and he says, "I am a handsome prince that has had a spell cast upon him; if you will kiss me it will break the spell and I will reappear. I will be so grateful that I will give you the best sex imaginable for the rest of your life." So she plants a large smooch on the frog, and guess what *she* turns into…the nearest motel!

HIGHER EDUCATION

54.

Monica Lewinsky returns home after the famous fiasco at the White House and announces that she has decided to go to medical school. Her father says, "I certainly don't think that's a good idea; as an intern you sucked."

SOME USEFUL SENTENCES TO KNOW
WHEN TRAVELING IN MOSLEM COUNTRIES

55.

AKHBAR KHALI-KILI HAFTIR LOTFAN
Thank you for showing me your marvelous gun.

FEKR GABUL CRADAN PAEH GUYSH DIVAR
I am delighted to accept your kind invitation to lie on the floor with my arms above my head and my legs apart.

SHOMAEH AUTO JEPHAHEH GHERMEZ BANDE
It is exceptionally kind of you to allow me to travel in the trunk of your car.
FASHAL-EH NA DEGAT MANO GAFTAM CHESHAYEH MOHEMARA
If you will do me the kindness of not harming my genital appendages, I will gladly reciprocate by betraying my country in public.

MATERNTER KHREL ALHEIEM, GHORBAN
The red blindfold will be lovely, Excellency.

TIEKHI NUNEH OB KHROLEM BEZORG VA INO BEGERAM
The water-soaked breadcrumbs are delicious, thank you. I must have the recipe.

MANEH MANEH MANEH
Whatever you say is fine.

FOSSILS

56.

Recent finds in the Jurassic Age digs in Montana have revealed an entirely new species of dinosaur all of which seem to be female specimens that have been determined to have had aberrant sexual preferences. Those at the dig conducted a name-finding contest, and the winner by unanimous vote was: LIKSALOTTAPUS.

THE FROGS

57.

Said the lezzie frog to her companion, "They're right. We do taste like chicken!"

THE GOOD MAN

58.

They say: If there's not a good woman behind a good man, there's no telling what the good man is behind.

BREAKDANCING

59.

Sources say: Breakdancing originated in New York City by black kids stealing hubcaps from moving vehicles.

SHIPWRECKED

60.

Picture, if you will…a very lonesome island nowhere near the shipping lanes. A thirtyish gent has been stranded there for a multitudinous numerousity of years when fate throws up on the shore a twentyfivish lady of pleasing face and form. He asks her what he might do for her, and she says she'd really like a hot shower. He proudly shows her that he has constructed a shower adjacent to his habitation and it even has hot water. After her shower he asks he what she would like to drink, and she responds "Martini, please," not really expecting that one might be available. She is surprised when he serves one up to her, explaining that the island very fortunately has the necessary ingredients growing in profusion. Nextly, he delights her by broiling a nice sirloin steak harvested by him from the bovine segment of the island's inhabitants. After dinner he asks he if she would like to play around, and she says, "You mean to say that you've actually built a golf course on this island?"

HIDE AND SEEK

61.

Girl: "Let's play hide and seek; if you find me you can have me!" Guy: "What if I can't find you?" Girl: "I'll be in the closet under the stairs!"

THE CARDINALS

62.

Here we have three Cardinals in heaven, an Italian, a Polack and a black. The first said that he originally was upset by the fact that the new Pope was not Italian, but added that he thought that he was okay. The Polack said that he was quite pleased that the new Pope was Polish and that it was greatly overdue to have a Polish Pope. The black then said, "I agree with what you say about the Pope, but I am concerned that there never has been a black Pope, and I wonder when that can be expected. At this a disembodied voice was heard to say in stentorian tones, "Not as long as I am God!"

THE TALENTED BIRD

63.

A preacher in our town acquired a parrot that was quite some talker, and the preacher decided to train the parrot to take part in church services. With great patience and perseverance he teaches the parrot to light the candles on his cue which is, "And the fire came down from heaven." When the parrot demonstrates that he can do this with great facility, the preacher springs his act on the congregation one Sunday. He says, "And the fire came down from heaven." Nothing happens, so he says it more loudly. The result is the same, so the preacher practically shouts, "AND THE FIRE CAME DOWN FROM HEAVEN!" At this the parrot squawks, just as loudly, "AND THE CAT PISSED ON THE MATCHES."

THE OPINION

64.

A lady up in Vermont near Burlington admitted that she never knew what her opinion was on the subject under discussion until she heard what she had to say about it.

CONCERNING WORDS

65.

The wise man tells us, "Profanity is the literary crutch of the inarticulate motherf—ker!"

AT THE SUMMIT

66.

FDR and Winston Churchill had a summit meeting in the Canary Islands shortly after the USA entered the war. FDR caught Churchill coming out of Eleanor's bedroom in the wee hours of the morning. He says, "Winston, I don't want to see any more of that!" And Churchill replies, "Neither do I, FDR...neither do I!"

THE CAMPAIGNER

67.

Truman was known for having injected religion into his campaign: he told everyone to go to hell!

THE PARADE

68.

St. Patrick's Day is the day the Jews go over to 5th Avenue to watch their employees march in a parade.

THE DRINKING BUDDIES

69.

Picture, if you will…two guys sitting at the bar indulging in consuming numerous redundancies of their favorite cocktail. One says, "Ya know what…I'm hungry." With this he fishes an olive from his martini and pops it into his mouth. He chews it thrice and his thoroughly crocked buddy says, "Ah! That calls for an after-dinner drink!"

A GREAT INVENTION

70.

Picture, if you will…Eli Whitney rushing into his house from his workshop. He grabs his wife and says, "Guess what, my sweet, I just invented the cotton gin!" To which his wife says, "Who would want a fluffy martini?"

FAIR PLAY

71.

Picture, if you will…a bunch of young kids out playing their games. A little girl comes into her house and asks her mother, "Mama, can I have a baby?" "No, dear", says her mother. The little girl then says, "Are you sure, Mama?" "Yes, dear I am sure." With this the little girl runs out to where her friends are romping and says, "O.K, guys, same game!"

THE PHEASANT PLUCKER

72.

I am a pheasant plucker, a pleasingly pleasant pheasant plucker; I pluck pheasant feathers. I am the most pleasingly pleasant pheasant feather plucker you'll ever meet.

AT THE DINER

73.

Picture, if you will…three guys at the counter of a diner type establishment. The counter lady, a large fat black woman takes their orders. Two order hamburgers, and the third orders a hot dog.

The black lady serve person goes to the fridge, takes out two hamburgers and proceeds to put one in each armpit, clamping her arms down to her sides. Upon inquiry of the customers who have ordered hamburgers, she explains that they cook faster if she warms them up a bit in her armpits as she has just demonstrated. With this the third guy says, "I don't think I'll take the hot dog; give me a ham sandwich, okay?"

THE MEDICATION

74.

Picture, if you will…a gay chap who has just come home from the drug store with a prescription that is in the form of suppositories. He undresses, takes a shower and proceeds to insert the suppository in the orifice designated in the prescription; he notices that he is getting an erection and says, "Don't be silly; it's only us!"

NOUVELLE FACE LIFT

75.

This lady we know had had so many face lifts that she had her cosmetic surgeon graft on to the back of her head a discreet knob which, when she turned it, stretched the skin of her face thus making her look younger and more attractive, she told herself. Time came for her periodic check-up, so she goes to her surgeon for a status exam. She acknowledges that she likes the idea of the knob, but, she says, "I'm concerned about these huge bags under my eyes." The doctor says, "Those aren't bags, my dear, they're your breasts." To this the lady says, "Oh! That explains the goatee!"

BOBBIT OFFSHOOT

76.

You certainly remember Lorena Bobbit, the famous personality who cut off her hubby's hoo-hoo and then left the premises with it, tossing the severed member out of her car window in the midst of her snit. Well…at the instant of that casual disposal of the result of her crude surgery there was a car coming from the opposite direction and the discarded hoo-hoo hit the windshield of the other car "SPLAT". There were two Polacks in that car, and one said to the other, "Boy, did you see the dick on that fly!"

IN MOURNING

77.

Picture, if you will…a widow lady with two grown children. She has been in deep mourning for an extended period of time. Her children, a boy and a girl, fervently wish that she might meet someone in whom she might get interested. They finally find a man, a widower of similar experiences, and they fix up a double blind date between the two of them. Well, they hit it off from the get go, so to speak, and it eventuates that she agrees to go up to the Catskills for a weekend.

After a romantic dinner with some wine, they retire to their suite. He disrobes, and so does she, that is, all but some black lace panties. She advises him that the panties are a symbol of her mourning and that she will not be taking them off in the forseeable future. She tells him that he can touch her here, here and here, but the panties stay on. He respects her feelings in this regard and accepts some hugging and cuddling for the nonce.

The next night she again disrobes before him, and the black lace panties stay on. He takes off his clothes and appears before her in all his erectile glory wearing nothing but a black condom. She asks him why the black condom, and he replies, "I am offering my condolences!"

FAMILY VALUES

78.

Picture, if you will…a two-man cell in a medium security state penitentiary. A 165 pound thirtyish white guy has just been placed in the cell already occupied for a long time by a 280 pound black guy; he is ferocious looking and not really very elegant or sweet smelling, if you get the picture.

The black guy says to the newcomer, "As you may know, my man, when two guys get thrown into a two-man cell togetha heah in the slamma they haz ta make a decision as to what direction they relationship gonna take. Now, you has gotch ta decide wheatha you iz gonna be de wife o' de husban'; ah'z givvin' you de choice.

Well, the newcomer thinks this over and has no desire to be the wife to this gigantic individual; he shudders to think what that would be like, so he says that he'll be the husband.

Whereupon, his big black cellmate says. "Da's fahn wi me; now you c'mon ovah heah and suck yo' wife's c—k!"

HEADLINE NEWS STORIES

79.

Sources say that the following headlines actually appeared in miscellaneous important newspapers in recent years; makes sense.

Astronaut Takes Blame for Gas in Spacecraft
Cold Wave Linked to Temperatures
War Dims Hope for Peace
Panda Mating Fails; Veterinarian Takes Over
Prostitutes Appeal to Pope
Drunk Gets Nine Months in Violin Case
Something Went Wrong in Jet Crash, Expert Says
Juvenile Court to Try Shooting Defendant
Miami Couple Slain; Police Suspect Homicide
Local High school Dropouts Cut in Half

Hospital Sued by 6 Foot Doctors
Chef Throws His Heart into Feeding Needy
Stolen Painting Found by Tree
Red Tape Holds up New Bridges
Storm Rips Through Cemetery; Hundreds Dead
New Obesity Study Looks for Larger Test Group
Man Hit by Lightning Faces Battery Charge
Plane Too Close to Ground, Crash Probe Told

UGLY

80.

My girl friend is so ugly that when I take her to the zoo I have to buy two tickets for her, one to get her in, and one to get her out.

BEATING INFLATION

81.

We know a girl who demolished inflation by selling another key to her apartment.

COMPASSION

82.

The scene is a courtroom, and the defendant is a recent widow. The Judge asks her, "Why did you kill your husband with a golf club?" She replies, "I didn't want to wake the kids."

BITS OF WISDOM

83.

A quadrasexual is a person who will do anything with anyone or any number of people for a quarter.

84.

Mother says that if sex was supposed to be fun, God wouldn't have included children as a penalty.

85.

There is a new airline operating between Geneva and various cities in Italy; it's name is Genitalia.

86.

Another new airlines, the result of a merger between El Al, the Isreali airline, and Alitalia; the emerging entity is named Val Italia.

TOO HAPPY

87.

Wife: "O'Brien has been drinking like that since I jilted him ten years ago."
Husband: "That's ridiculous; I don't care what the reason, ten years is too long to celebrate.

IN THE CONFESSIONAL

88.

"Bless me, Father for I have sinned; I killed a politician."
Priest: I don't want to hear about your community service work; I'm here to listen to your sins."

THE DRINK

89.

Man to his host: "Do lemons have feathers?" "No!" replies his host. "Then I think I squeezed your canary into my gin and tonic!"

THE LAWYER

90.

A lawyer accepted a $100 fee from an elderly client. After the man had left the lawyer noticed that two $100 bills were stuck together. With this he had a moral dilemma: should he tell his partner?

FORMERLY SINGLE

91.

Wife says, "Before we got married, you said you were well off." Says he, "I was, but I didn't know it!"

THE WEDDING NIGHT

92.

Young man to bride on wedding night as they hop into bed: "Don't look for too much experience from me."
Bride replies, "Okay, dear, just so you don't look for too much virginity from me."

SPLIT?

93.

"My wife would get a divorce if she could figure out how to do it without making me happy."

THE WRESTLERS

94.

Picture, if you will…the aftermath of a very closely contested wrestling match. A guy is congratulating the winner, a good friend. "Fantastic, Joe, I thought for a minute you were a sure gonner; what happened?" "Well," says Joe, "I did too; he had me all tied up in a knot; I didn't know which end was up. I was about to toss in the towel, so to speak, when I saw a pair of balls staring me in the face, I figured I had nothing to lose, so I bit them as hard as I could, and that did it; the knot immediately became untangled, and I was the winner. You can't imagine what superhuman strength you can summon by biting yourself in the nuts!"

THE DENTIST

95.

Picture, if you will…an uptown cocktail lounge where singles mingle. An attractive young man and a foxy chick establish contact and have a few drinks. They are getting along famously, as they say, and it eventuates that she asks him to go over to her place for additional conversation on topics of mutual interest, and he does so. At her apartment they have additional drinks and one thing leads to another, as they say, and they repair to her bedroom. He takes off his shirt and then washes his hands; he takes off his pants and briefs and washes his hands again. She says, "You must be a dentist." He replies, "That's right. How did you know?" She says. "Dentists are always washing their hands." He says, "That's very perceptive of you; I'm impressed." At this juncture, they proceed to make love, and while later experiencing the afterglow she says, "You must be a really good dentist." He says, "Well, as a matter of fact I am regarded as being a very good dentist; how did you reach that conclusion? To which she replies, "I hardly felt anything at all!"

THE AFTER LIFE

96.

This concerns a thirty-ish couple, very close, very much in love. They are believers in spiritual matters and reincarnation and the like and make a pact that if and when one of them dies the other will make a sincere effort to communicate with the decedent exactly 30 days after his or her death. Well, it happens that the guy is killed in an auto accident sometime later, and on the thirtieth day after his demise, she attempts, successfully, to get in touch with her dear departed. She is elated to hear him answer her plea and says, "Tell me, dear, what is it like?" He says, "It's beautiful; the sky is blue, the sun is out, humidity is low and my routine is quite pleasurable: I awaken at about nine and make love from then 'til noon; have a bite, and a short nap, following which I make love until suppertime.

Then after supper I make love 'til about eleven and then go to sleep." She says, "Oh that's marvelous, heaven sounds like a perfect place." He says, "I'm not in heaven, dear; I'm a rabbit in Southern California!"

THE ENCHANTED

97.

Once upon a time in a land far from here a beautiful young maiden was sitting by a peaceful pond looking at a bevy of transient ducks when a frog jumped into her lap and said, "I am the victim of a spell cast upon me by a wicked witch. If you kiss me I'll turn back into the handsome young prince that I am. And then, my beautiful one we can marry, set up housekeeping in yon castle with my mother where you can prepare my meals, clean and mend my clothes, bear my children and forever feel grateful and happy doing so."

That night in her apartment while enjoying a repast of lightly sauteed frog legs, seasoned in a garlic, butter and white wine sauce, she thought of the events of the afternoon and, chuckling to herself, thought "I don't f—king think so…"

MARKET RESEARCH

98.

A market researcher knocks on a suburban door; it opens, and there stands a young woman with three little girls hanging onto her skirt. He says, "I'm doing some market research for the folks that make Vaseline; are you familiar with that product?" "Oh, yes," says the young woman, "my husband and I use it all the time." Do you mind telling me what you use it for?" "Not at all; we use it for sex." The researcher is surprised at this frank answer and says, I appreciate your candor; most people lie to me and say that they use if on a bicycle chain or to lubricate a hinge on the gate; do you mind telling me just how you use it for sex?" The lady says, "I don't mind telling you; we put it on the doorknob; it keeps the kids out of the bedroom when we're fooling around."

THE LITTLE HELPER

99.

A young couple with their 6-year-old daughter have moved into a new neighborhood; next door is a vacant lot upon which a crew is building a new house. The little girl understandably takes a great interest in what is going on next door and starts talking to the construction guys. She hangs around a lot, and soon the guys develop a good deal of affection for her and more or less adopt her as the project mascot. They let her sit with them during coffee breaks and at lunch time and give her little jobs for her to do to make her feel important. At the end of the first week they even give her a pay envelope with a dollar bill in it. This she takes immediately to her mother who trots her off to the bank to open an account so she can learn about money and the importance of saving. The teller thinks that this is really cute and asks her where she got the dollar. To this the little girl says proudly, "I have been helping the workers build a house all week." The teller says, "My goodness; that's awesome, and will you be working on the house this week too?" "I will if those useless c—ksuckers down at the lumberyard ever bring us the f—kin' wood," replies the little girl."

HEED THE SIGNS

100.

The following signs and notices have been observed by the traveling American, namely, viz and to wit:

In an Austrian hotel catering to the ski crowd: "Not to perambulate the corridors during the hours of repose in the boots of ascension."

In a Danish airline ticket office: "We collect your bags and send them in all directions."

From a Japanese information booklet about the hotel air conditioning made available to American guests: "Cooles and Heates. If you want just condition of warm, please control yourself."

In a Belgrade hotel elevator: "To move the cabin, push button of wishing floor. If the cabin should enter more persons, each one should push button of wishing floor. Driving is then going alphabetically by national order."

From a brochure of a car rental company in Tokyo: "When a passenger of foot heave in sight, tootle the horn. Trumpet him melodiously at first, but if he still obstancles your passage, then tootle him with vigor."

Sign in Tokyo hotel: "You are invited to take advantage of the chambermaid."

In the lobby of a Bucharest hotel: "The lift is being fixed for the next day. During that time we regret that you will be unbearable."

THE RED VS. THE GREEN

101.

Picture, if you will...a doctor's waiting room; two men are there waiting to see the doctor about their respective individual medical problems. They get to chatting, and after revealing what brings each to the doctor's office, it appears that one has a red ring at the base of his hoo-hoo, and the other has a green ring similarly located on his person.

The first is called in to see the doctor, and after a few minutes, as he passes through the waiting room, he says, "Don't worry, chum; it's nothing." At this point the other is notified that the doctor is ready to see him and proceeds to the examination room. He shows the doc the green ring at the base of his caudal appendage, and the doctor says, "Hmmm, this is serious!"

The patient is visibly shaken and relates to the doctor that the other fellow with a similar manifestation told him that it wasn't anything to worry about.

"Well," says the doctor, "There's a big difference between lipstick and gangrene."

AT THE GALLERY

102.

Picture, if you will…an art gallery in Coconut Grove; an important new show has just been hung, and the members of the public that go in for this sort of thing are milling about drinking the jug wine that is being dispensed. Two ladies are seated on a bench contemplating a large painting labeled "Early Afternoon". Depicted in the painting before them are three nude black guys sitting on a crude wooden bench; the one in the middle has a pink hoo-hoo. The ladies are trying to relate the name of the painting to the subjects displayed, and they are encountering some difficulty.

At this point the artist comes over and says, "I am the man who did this painting; is there anything you'd like to know about it; you have puzzled expressions, if you don't mind my saying."

The ladies respond, practically in unison, "We are having trouble understanding the title of the painting; here we have three naked negroes sitting on a bench, the one in the middle has a pink hoo-hoo, and the title is 'Early Afternoon'".

"Oh, I see what your problem is: these are not African Americans depicted; they are coal miners in West Virginia, and the one in the middle went home for lunch."

GOTTA KEEP MOVIN'

103.

Picture, if you will…the maternity ward of the county hospital. An elderly gent is in the waiting room expecting to hear that his young wife has given birth to their child. The doctor appears with the news that a son has been born, and the doctor sees that the father is noticeably fidgeting and waving his arms about rhythmically as he receives the news, so he inquires of the latter why all the activity.

The man says, "I'm kinda old, ya see, and my wife is sorta young. I gotta keep movin'; gotta keep my engine revvin' ta keep up with her." The doctor gets the point, and life goes on.

The following year the elderly gent in question is back in the waiting room on a similar scenario waiting for the birth of their second child. Again, he is fidgeting and waving his arms about in the same manner as a year earlier, once more explaining that he has to keep his motor running to keep up with his young wife. Again the doctor nods understandingly.

The next year the process and activity is repeated, and as before, he tells the doctor that he still has his motor running as proven by three babies in three years, to which the doctor says "Well, sir, I know what you mean when you say that you've kept your motor running, but I suggest that perhaps you should get an oil change; this one's black!"

AT THE BANK

104.

Picture, if you will...your friendly neighborhood sperm bank. Seated at a desk is a woman who is being confronted by a guy wearing a ski mask and holding a handgun. He says to her, "Pick up that jar of semen there on your desk and let me see you drink it all...straight down." The woman gags at the thought, but she is afraid of the gun and does as she is ordered. After she has delicately wiped off her chin, he rips off the ski mask, and she sees that it is her husband, who says, "There, that wasn't so bad was it?"

THOUGHT PROVOKERS

105.

If a mute swears, does his mother wash his hands with soap?

If a man is standing in the middle of a forest speaking and there is no woman around to hear him, is he still wrong?

Is there another word for synonym?

Would a fly without wings be called a walk?

Is it true that cannibals don't eat clowns because they taste funny?

Do pediatricians play miniature golf on Wednesdays?

What does one say when God sneezes?

If you try to fail, and succeed, which have you done?

Before they invented drawing boards, what did they go back to? Maybe, "square one?"

If the #2 pencil is the most popular, why is it still #2?

Where do forest rangers go to "get away from it all"?

If someone with multiple personalities threatens to kill himself, is it a hostage situation?

Why is it called "tourist season" if you can't shoot them?

I went to a bookstore and asked the saleswoman, "Where's the self-help section?" She said if she told me it would defeat the purpose?

What should you do if you see an endangered animal eating an endangered plant?

If the police arrest a mime, do they tell him that he has the right to remain silent?

If all the world's a stage, where is the audience sitting?

If one synchronized swimmer drowns, do the rest of them have to drown too?

How do they get the deer to cross at the yellow road sign?

Can vegetarians eat animal crackers?

A FEW WORDS OF WISDOM

106.

Atheism is a non-prophet concept.

One nice thing about egotists: they don't talk about other people.

Women like silent men; they think they are listening.

Age is a high price to pay for maturity.

Never underestimate the power of stupid people in large groups.

PERIPHRASTICALLY SPEAKING

107.

Feathered bi-ped vertebrates are gregarious according to their respective plumages.

A gyrotational fragment of lapidified material rotating on its axis will not agglomerate bryophytic vegetation.

All that scintillates is not, *ipso facto*, auriferous.

When the absence of the domesticated carniverous feline has been established, the diminutive residential rodents display a tendency to cavort.

Persons possessing an excess of ineptitudinousity, mental or physical, in evaluating correct procedures, impetuously itinerate into venues which predominately spiritual beings view with trepidation.

Avoid becoming involved in permanentification with respect to the numerousity of your barnyard fowl prior to their emergency from the protective capsulation in which they exist at the time of emergency from the parent.

Products of ingenious character are the offspring of exigency.

It's a longitudinous pathway that is devoid of any sinuational aspect.

A plethora of culinary specialists skilled in the preparation of gastronomic concoctions will tend to have a deleterious effect on the quality of a certain potable solution made by immersing a gallinaceous avis in a receptacle of seething irrigant.

Persisting in a virtually constant and prolonged exertion of a physical or intellectual character causes Jack to become a youth blunted in perception and sensibility.

The feathered biped vertebrate that betimely deserts the coziness of its abode acquires exclusive dominion and control over the vermiculatum.

Those who perforce are constrained to be domiciled in vitreous habitations of patent frangibility should refrain from employing petrous formations as projectiles.

One should hyperesthetically exercise macrography upon that venue that one will eventually tenant if one proposes to launch himself into the troposphere.

An intellectually challenged numbskull and his specie divaricate with conspicuous prematurity.

Aberration is the hallmark of Homo Sapiens, while longaminous placability and condonation are the indicia of supramundane omniscience.

Do not dissipate your competence with hebetudinous prodigality lest you subsequently lament an exiguous inadequacy.

It can be no other than a maleficent horizontally propelled current of atmospheric gases whose portentous advent is not the harbinger of a modicum of beneficence.

ANOTHER "WHAT D'YA GET..."

108.

What d'ya get when you cross an oversexed girl with an elephant?
You get a two-ton nympho who does it for peanuts...and never forgets you.

REALLY SUCCESSFUL SURGERY

109.

Picture, if you will...a thirtyish woman who is in the hospital to have the outer labia of her vulva surgically removed to cure a rare syndromical condition the name of which escapes me.

She is in the recovery room and has just emerged from the effects of the anesthesia. Her surgeon is by her bed and says, "Well, my dear, I have good news twice-over for you: firstly, the operation was completely successful; we have corrected the condition, and you have nothing further to worry about. Secondly, you see the two dozen roses over there in that vase? They are from the gentleman in the room directly above you who thanks you for his new ears."

THE VISUALLY CHALLENGED CASHIER

110.

Picture, if you will...a fortyish lady in a BIG K-MART. She has just brought to the checkout counter a fishing rig that has been advertised at 40% off. While waiting in line she notices that the cashier apparently is blind, yet he seems to be competently handling the duties of his position. When her turn comes she is a little unsure as to just what she should do.

He perceives a certain hesitancy on her part and says, "Yes, Madam, I am blind, but this store believes in employing sight-challenged persons who are able to do their assigned jobs. I have developed my own way of handling this job. I have familiarized myself with the prices of the various items in the store including those that are on sale today. Just drop your purchase here on the counter, and I'll be able to tell you what its price is.

She is amazed of course and places her rod-and-reel combo on the counter; whereupon, the blind cashier says, "This is a Frenaye fishing rod replete with a Halliburton no-tangle, anti-backlash reel with 400 feet of nylon monofilament line, and it's on sale for $40.00." This happens to be accurate, so her amazement is compounded and complete.

Just then the cashier gets a phone call, excuses himself and talks briefly. While he is thus engaged the lady rather noisily breaks wind.

The blind cashier punches buttons on his cash register and says, "Madam, that will be $48.50." To this she says, "You just acknowledge that this fishing combination was on sale for $40.00; now you try to charge me $48.50; I'm afraid I don't understand." "Yes, Madam, that is correct; the fishing gear is $40.00; then there's the duck call for $6.00 and $2.50 for the fish bait."

IT'S ALL RELATIVE

111.

Picture, if you will…a retired British Army Colonel on a double-decker bus in Soho, that is, London, England. Across the aisle is a weird looking young dude sporting a Mohawk haircut dyed blue, red, yellow and green. The Col. Is fascinated and finds himself staring at this multicolored teenager.

The weird dude becomes aware of the attention he is getting from the Colonel and says, "Wot the bloody hell you lookin' at Guv'nor?" To which the latter says, "Years ago in India as a young Leftenant I had an affair with a parrot; I thought for a minute you might be my Grandson!"

SHADES OF CONTACT

112.

Picture, if you will…a fortune teller's parlor; seated at the table is a ventriloquist wearing the customary turban and cloak. Business is bad in his usual occupation as a ventriloquist, so he has turned to the telling of fortunes to keep body and soul together.

On the other side of the table is a lady who has recently lost her husband. She questions him concerning the cost of a séance. He says, "That depends; if you hear your husband's voice in the course of the séance, that will be five pounds. It will be ten pounds if you have a lengthy conversation with him, and twenty pounds if you converse with him while I'm drinking a glass of water."

THE SINGING CANARY

113.

Picture, if you will…a man walking by a pet shop. He hears a beautiful bird-song emanating from the premises. He is enthralled; he has to have that bird; he has never heard anything quite like it. He goes in and speaks to the proprietor, "I just heard your bird singing; I'm interested in acquiring that bird; I have to have it! Money is no object!"

The proprietor says, "Well I will sell him to you for the sticker price, and I'm pleased that you appreciate his singing." With this, the Proprietor goes into the back room from whence cometh the trilling and returns with the bird in question on a perch singing his little brains out. He notices with some dismay that the bird has only one leg, and points out this anatomical deficiency to the shop owner, disappointment being evident in his voice. To this, the proprietor says, "Well make up your mind, Mister, do you want a singer or a dancer?"

THE POOR GUY

114.

Picture, if you will...two guys talking about their early days. One asks the other, "Tell me; were you poor when you were a lad?"

"Was I poor, you ask? Well, let me tell you about that. We were so poor that we used to get Care packages from Haiti! How about you?"

The first replies, "We were very poor also; my father couldn't afford to buy me a suit, but he was so proud that he didn't want anyone to know about it, so he bought me a nice hat and let me look out the window."

THE GOOD MARRIAGE

115.

Picture, if you will...a nice Jewish couple; they have three nice boys. They grow up in a household where the Jewish religion is an integral part of every day life. It is instilled in them that they will make their parents very happy if they marry nice Jewish girls.

The eldest happens to fall madly in love and elope with a beautiful Catholic girl named Kelly O'Brien. The parents are nearly devastated, so they go to work on the two remaining sons hoping they will bring home Jewish brides.

The next eldest falls hopelessly in love with a Greek Orthodox girl named Kapadopolous, so he, too is gone. Now there is just Hymie left, and in due course he succumbs to the charms of a woman and elopes with her. Imagine the parents delight when he calls from Niagara Falls and tells them he has married a girl whose last name is Goldberg. They are ecstatic! Then the father asks what her first name is and the son says, "Whoopie, Junior!"

AT THE HOME

116.

Picture, if you will...an old folks home. An upper-middle-aged couple is visiting his elderly father who has been staying at the home for the last few months. They interrogate him about the details of his everyday life, and he tells them, among other things, that each night when he is ready to retire to his bed a man comes around and gives him a cup of hot chocolate and a Viagra pill.

They immediately search out the manager of the place and confront him with the revelation that they have received from his father, and the manager confirms that the information is correct. "Do you mean to tell us that you give my 82-

year-old father a Viagra pill every night?" says the man. "Yes, we do," replies the other, "they have determined from extensive research that this is quite effective."

"What do you mean 'effective'? This is a single man with no possible romantic entanglement." "Well," says the other, "it *is* effective; it keeps him from falling out of bed!"

A SIGNIFICANT EVENT

117.

Goldberg finds himself in a Fortune Teller's parlour. She gazes into the crystal ball and tells him, "One thing I can tell you right now: you will die on a Jewish holiday."

"What Jewish holiday?" he asks.

"Doesn't matter," she replies, "the day you die will be a Jewish holiday!"

NO MORE CIGARS

118.

The White House physician has prescribed that William Jefferson Clinton give up cigars. It seems that he had developed a yeast infection!

THE AGGRESSOR

119.

Picture, if you will…that part of the male anatomy wherein sperm is born. There is one sperm in particular that seems to be most anxious to be the first one to nail an ovum should circumstances develop along that line. One evening the sperm in question gets a signal that it seems likely that he will get his chance, because sexual stimulation has indicated that he and the others are about to go to work, so to speak. Things get more frantic, and our aggressive sperm is swimming madly up the phallic duct ready to beat out all the others that actually are not very far behind him. Suddenly, he stops and turns back, swimming against the flow, shouting, "Go back! Go back! It's just a blow job!"

GEOGRAPHICAL REALITY

120.

Picture, if you will…two woodpeckers in the Dallas area. One lives there, and the other is visiting from Anchorage, Alaska. The Texas bird says, "I'm glad you're here; it will give a you a chance to try out some of our trees. In fact, we have one native tree here that none of us local guys can put a dent in; would you like to give it a try?"

The visitor expresses interest in accepting the challenge, and to the chagrin of the Dallas bird, the Alaska woodpecker demolishes the tree in question virtually to sawdust in a matter of minutes.

It then comes to pass that the Texas bird subsequently make a visit to the habitat of the Alaska woodpecker and upon that occasion is advised by his host that they have a tree up there that the local woodpeckers have been unable to peck effectively, similar to the situation that the Dallas bird had previously exposed at his home base.

Well, the visiting woodpecker is eager to take up the challenge thus presented, and to the amazement of the Alaska contingent the visitor swiftly converts the tree in question to chips, in a manner of speaking.

The moral of this story must be obvious by now, namely, viz and to wit: Your pecker is always a lot harder when you are away from home!

THE VIRGIN? BRIDE

121.

Picture, if you will…a man who has all the money he could possibly ever hope to spend. In other words, with him, money is no object. He decides that he wants to marry a virgin, and being cynical but realistic he figures that if he starts out with a young female child and engineers her upbringing and education in a careful way he can marry her when she becomes of age, and she will be a virgin.

So he finds a five-year-old girl, has her examined by a physician who certifies that she qualifies and is in perfect health. He then places her in a convent school which has a reputation as an institution of excellence in education and discipline. The nuns love the little girl and she them. Her patron visits her regularly and sees to it that she is happy where she is.

She develops into a beautiful young lady, and when she has completed the junior high school curriculum, he arranges for her to enter a prestigious Catholic School in a monastery in the Swiss Alps noted for the intellectual character of the education therein dispensed. Her patron inspects the institution in question and is convinced that this is the place where she should complete her education and training.

When she attains the age of 18 years, he takes her from the monastery to Paris where he shows her everything Paris has to offer: the best food, the finest champagnes…everything. He tells her that he loves her and wants her to marry him. She accepts his proposal and tells him that everything she is she owes to him, that she is very fond of him and in time she knows that she will grow to love him dearly. Based on this they marry.

Finally, the time comes for the deflowering that he has planned for so long. They are in bed, and he is ready. He picks up a tube of K-Y Jelly and prepares to lubricate his member so that the invasion of her person will be less painful. She asks him what it is that he is going to do with what is in the tube. He explains that he is going to put his member into her vagina and this will make the entry a lot smoother and less painful. To this the sweet little girl whose complete life he has arranged, says, "Why don't you just spit on your dick like the monks do?"

THE CAJUN HUNTER

122.

(Should be told with a Cajun accent, if possible.)

Picture, if you will…Boudreau getting into his pirogue early one morning; he has a large roll of silver duct tape in his hand and a big burlap poke hanging over his shoulder. His friend, Thibedeau observes this little tableau an' say, "Boudreau, whey you goin' wi' dat duct tape an' this poke this mo'nin'?"

Boudreau, he answer, "I goin' duck huntin' in next bayou, whey I goin', das wot. You lak come wi' me? Get lotsa ducks fo' sho'; dat's wha I got dis duck tape wi' me." Thibedeau thinks Boudreau is nuts, so he declines with thanks but no thanks. He has things to do.

Well, Boudreau, he come back dat evenin' an' he have 'bout 12 nice ducks. Thibedeau see dis and wonders wot dis worl' comin' to, he do'.

Nex' day Thibedeau see Boudreau getting into his pirogue an' he have wi' him another big poke and a big box of Nutra-Sweet. When questioned by his friend, he, Boudreau, say, "I'm goin' huntin' nutria today, wi' dis nutra sweet, an' I'm goin' to put dem in this poke, I am. You wanta come wi' me, Thibedeau?" As before, his friend declines.

Sho 'nuff dat evenin' Boudreau he show up back at the dock w' de poke fulla nutria, an' his frien' shake his head, wonderin'.

Nex' day Thibedeau observes Boudreau getting' into his pirogue wi' a big poke and a bunch of pussy willows, and he say, "Wait, Boudreau, I wanna come wi' you today, I do."

A CAJUN STORY

123.

The scene is the Cajun County, West of New Orleans: Abbeville, New Roads, Cairncrow, LaFayette.

Boudreau sees his old friend, Hebert. "Hey, man, how you been?" "I been fine; how about you?" "Great hey, we ain't been for drinks at the hotel in LaFayette in long time! Hell, let's do it, man…OK?"

"See ya there tomorrow, both drive ya hear! OK!"

Next scene: Bar at the Hotel after six-seven sazeracs Boudreau does say, "I going home now, on I-10. See you later, Hebert; fine, man."

Out on I-10 Boudreau in his car, doin' 65. Police done fly by him, stop another car a mile ahead. Boudreau scared, man! He pull off on grass about 200 yards behind. He watch officer get out car, go to driver with speed-ticket book. Police look in back seat of car, sees knives, swords hatchets on seat. He pulls his gun and say, "Get out of car!" Man say "What's the matter?" Cop say, "I see you got big problems with all these weapons." Man say, "Officer, those aren't weapons; I'm a juggler; I do an act in the hotel."

Cop say, "You better damn sure you can juggle…get your ass out the car and show me!" Man gets out and does great act behind his car…weapons in the air, between his legs and all.

Boudreau he been watching this. He is now panicky, puts car in gear, does a U-turn across the median, speeds back to LaFayette Hotel, grabs his buddy Hebert by the arm and say, "Hebert, don't drive home on I-10 tonight, Man, you hear!!"

"Why you say that, Boudreau?" And Boudreau, he say, "Because, Man, they got a new DUI test you ain't gonna pass!!!"

<u>LEWINSKY/KACZYNSKI LIMERICK CONTEST</u>

124.

The following limericks are the top three entries in the contest held at the Black Rose Pub in Boston, MA. The contest requirements: to use the names Lewinsky and Kaczynski in a limerick.

Entry #1:
There once was a gal named Lewinsky
Who played on a flute like Stravinsky.
   'Twas "Hail to the Chief"
   On the flute made of beef
That stole the front page from Kaczynski.

Entry #2:
   Said Clinton to young Ms. Lewinsky
   Let's not leave clues like Kaczynski
      Since you look such a mess,
      Use the hem of your dress,
   And wipe that stuff off of your chinsky.

Entry #3:
   Lewinsky and Clinton have shown
   What Kaczynski must surely have known:
      That an intern is better
      Than a bomb in a letter,
  Given the choice to be blown.

PFIZER STRIKES AGAIN AND AGAIN

125.

It is rumored that Pfizer is planning to come out with several new drugs oriented toward improving the performance of men in today's society:

DIRECTRA – In a clinical trial a dose of this drug given to men prior to leaving on car trips caused 73 percent of them to stop and ask directions when they got lost, compared to a control group of 0.2%.

NEGA-VIAGRA – Has the exactly opposite effect of VIAGRA. Currently undergoing clinical trials on sitting or recently prior U.S. Presidents. (Depending on time considerations at publication.)

NEGA-SPORTAGRA – This experimental drug has the strange effect of making men want to turn off televised sports and actually converse with other family members.

FLYAGRA – This drug has shown great promise in treating men with O.F.D. (Open-Fly Disorder). Especially useful for men on VIAGRA.

LIAGRA – This drug causes men to be less than candid when being asked about their sexual affairs. It will be available in Regular, Grand Jury and Presidential strengths.

THE PIOUS PARROT

126.

The owner of the pet store calls up the Episcopal Minister to tell him that he has a parrot that might interest him. His curiosity aroused, the cleric goes over to the pet store to scope out the parrot in question. The proprietor says, "You should find this parrot interesting; with him you can spice up your sermons. You'll notice that there is a string tied to each of his legs. If you pull the one on the left leg, the parrot will recite the Lord's Prayer, and if you pull the string tied to his right leg he recites the 23rd Psalm." "What happens," says the the clergyman, "if you pull both of the strings at the same time?" Here the parrot steps in, "I fall on my ass, is what!"

AWAY AT SCHOOL

127.

Letter from son, away at school:

Dear Dad:

$school is really great. There'$ lot$ to do and I am $tudying very hard. I like my new friend$, and with all my $tuff, I $imply can't think of a thing I need, so if you like, you can ju$t $end me a card, a$ I would love to hear from you. Love, Your $on.

The reply:

Dear Son:

I kNOw that astroNOmy, ecoNOmics, and OceaNOgraphy are eNOugh to keep even an hoNOr student like you busy. Do NOt forget, acquiring kNOwledge is a NOble task, and you can never study eNOugh. Love, Dad.

THE SUPERNATURAL

128.

Picture, if you will...a lecture hall at a prominent university. A prof is speaking to a large group of students on the subject of the supernatural. He asks for a show of hands from all those who believe in ghosts. About ninety students raise their hands. "Well, that's a good start; now of you all, how many think you have seen a ghost?" 40 hands. "Talked to a ghost?" 15 hands. "Ever touched a ghost?" 3 hands. "That's fantastic! But let's take this a step further; have any of you ever made love to a ghost?" A single hand goes up in the back of the hall, a guy in a plaid shirt and a Braves baseball cap. The prof is clearly boggled of the mind and says, "Son, in all the years I have been giving this lecture no one has ever claimed to have done it with a ghost. Come on up here and tell us about your experience." The redneck student starts forward with a grin on his face, and as he approaches the podium the professor says, "O.K., son, tell us what it's like to have sex with a ghost." To which the student replies, "Ghost?! Sheeyit, from back there it sounded like you were talkin' about 'Goats'."

IT'S BASEBALL

129.

Picture, if you will...a Scotsman who has traveled to the states and is attending his first baseball game. He knows nothing about the game. The first batter gets a hit, and the crowd yells, "Run man, run!" The next batter also gets a hit, and the Scotsman yells, "run man, run". He is really enjoying himself and every time a batter gets a hit he yells, "Run man, run." Finally, reality strikes, and a batter gets 1, 2, 3, 4 balls drops his bat and starts to walk to first base; as before, the Scotsman yells, "Run man, run." The gentleman next to him says, "No, no, he doesn't run; he walks; he has four balls." To this the Scotsman yells, "Walk proudly, son, walk proudly."

THE BALLOONIST

130.

O'Brien decided to take up ballooning...heard it was quite exciting. One day he was up there in the sky and found himself in a bit of a pickle, so to speak: he was coming in to the land mass from the sea and a layer of clouds developed below him. Naturally he was concerned; this was something new for which he had not received instruction. Then suddenly through a hole in the cloud layer, and he spotted a farmer down below plowing a field. He hollered as loudly as he could, "Ahoy, down there; where am I?" To which the farmer hollered back, "Ya can't fool me; you're up there in that little basket!"

THE ANATOMY CLASS

131.

Picture, if you will…an anatomy class that has just convened for the hour assigned. The teacher is perusing the homework that has been turned in by her students that morning. She calls on one of the girls, "Janice, get up and tell the class what part of the human body enlarges to seven times its size when stimulated." Janet stands up and says that she is too embarrassed to answer that question. The teacher says, "Sit down, Janice; Robert, you tell us the answer." He arises and says, "That's an easy one; the pupil of the eye enlarges to seven times its size when stimulated." The teacher says, "That's the correct answer, Robert. And, Janet, first of all, you didn't do your homework; secondly, you have a dirty mind, and thirdly, when you get married, you're going to be sadly disappointed!"

THE HARD WAY

132.

One night a traveling salesman seeks an overnight at a farmhouse out in the country when his car breaks down. The farmer is very hospitable and says, "Wal, don't have a room for ya here in the house, but gotta barn fulla hay; ya kin sleep thar; think yu'll find that cumferbul." So he sleeps in the hayloft. The next morning he hears the rooster and wakes up to see the farmer entering the barn. He thanks the farmer for putting him up and tells him that he has just had the best night's sleep in years. He then watches the farmer taking hay from the barn to the milk cows, but it is strange the way the farmer is going about it: first the farmer climbs the ladder to the hayloft with a pitchfork on his shoulder, then he takes a forkful of hay, puts it over his shoulder and climbs down to the floor of the barn and carries the hay about 20 yards to the cows. The salesman watches this for a bit and then says, "Why don't you just pitch the hay down from the hayloft to the floor instead of all this climbing up and down?" The farmer says, "I like ta do things the hard way." So the salesman shrugs his shoulders philosophically, and goes out into the farmyard where he observes the farmer out by the well with a bucket in hand. The farmer climbs over the lip of the well and descends into the void on rungs built into the inside wall of the well. A few minutes later the farmer emerges from the well with the bucket of water which he gives to the chickens. The salesman says, "Why don't you rig up a rope-and-pulley arrangement in the well so you don't have to climb down each time you want some water? Be a lot easier on you?" "I like ta do things the hard way," says the farmer. Just then a stupefyingly gorgeous girl emerges from the house to feed the chickens some corn. The salesman has never seen a more naturally beautiful girl in his life. He says to the farmer, "Who's that?" And the farmer says, "That's m'daughter; right purty ain't she?" The other says, "Pretty? I think she is drop-dead gorgeous! And I'll bet that's something you didn't get the hard way." To which the farmer says, "Shore did...standin' up in a canoe!"

THE ALIBIS

133.

Sources say that it eventuated in a small town in Northern New York State that an unmarried lady was advised by her physician that she was with child. She told the doctor that he must be mistaken; she said "Can't be; I've never been with any man, it's impossible...unless a man snuck up on me while I was asleep." So, of course, this became her public excuse and, of course, the chief topic of gossip in the community. And on the Tuesday following the breaking of the item, the one-table Tuesday Afternoon Bridge Group considered the juicy topic. One lady said, "It couldn'a been my Albert; he was over to Rochester attending the Legion convention at that time." Another of the ladies said, "Well I know twasn't my Henry; he was in Chicago on that big produce conference at the time." A third lady said, "Well I know it wasn't my Harold; he was over ta Boston then." "Well," said the fourth lady, "I know 'tweren't my Elmer; if 'twere it'ud awoke her!"

PREGNANT

134.

Picture, if you will...a streetcar; all the seats are taken. A standing lady says to a young man who has claimed a seat, "Excuse me, young man, but would you give up your seat to a pregnant woman?" He jumps right up and says, "Certainly, Ma'am." She thanks him and sits down. The young man looks her over carefully and is unable to detect any sign of pregnancy, so he says, "Excuse me, Ma'am, but how long have you been pregnant?" She replies, "About thirty minutes, and *BOY*, am I tired.!"

MESSIN' AROUND

135.

Picture, if you will...a black guy, Leroy, and a girl he knows, Shandra Lou, who is quite attractive all over. He has a hankering to "do it" with her and approaches her on the subject. She says, "Cost ya." He says, "How much we talkin' 'bout?" "One dollah." He examines the contents of his pocket and says, "Only gots a quarta heah." She says, "Fo' a quarta all you kin do is mess aroun' a little." So Leroy remits the 25-cent piece and starts messin' aroun'. Well. one thing leads to another and Shandra Lou starts getting a little aroused. She whispers in Leroy's closest ear, "Leroy, you devil, Ah finds that ah'm gonna hafta lend you semty-fahv cents!"

NOBODY'S PERFECT

136.

Each one of us is a mixture of good qualities and some not-so-good qualities. In considering our fellow man we should remember his good qualities and realize that his faults only prove the he is, after all, a human being. We should refrain from making harsh judgment of a person just because he happens to be a dirty, rotten, sleazy, no-good rectal aperture.

WRONG SOLUTION

137.

Picture, if you will…a lady that has just been forced up against a wall by a dog with a really great set of fangs; she is conspicuously terrified, pissed-off and upset. The man who owns the dog comes running up; he says, "Don't worry about my dog; he's been neutered." She replies, "I knew from a block away that he wasn't going to f—k me; why didn't you get his teeth pulled?"

OLD ENGLISH PROVERB

138.

Young persons possessing above-average intelligence should consider entering the ministry, unless when they attend the university they are given to drinking, carousing and wenching, in which case, they ought to take up the study of law.

HAVE A DRINK

139.

Informed sources say that God gave us liquor so ugly girls can get laid too.

THE GAY RECRUITER

140.

Picture, if you will…two gays discoursing; one says, "Did you know that heterosexual intercourse causes cancer?" The other responds: "No; does it really?" "No," says the first…"but spread it around."

YOUNG AT HEART

141.

A man was arrested the other day; he was charged with fraud for selling rejuvenation pills. In due course, and in accordance with their policy the police looked up his record and discovered that he had been prosecuted for the same offense in 1907…1872…1753…1612.

AN EMOTIONAL EVENT

142.

The invitation to the party read, "Come dressed as an emotion."

One girl came dressed all in red; she said her emotion was Rage.

Another girl came all in green; her emotion was envy.

A black guy showed up in the nude, his hoo-hoo in the state of erection. Hanging from the end of his caudal appendage was a pear. His emotion, he said, "Is f—king despair."

HUMILIATION

143.

It's a terrible thing to be arrested for indecent exposure...and then be released for insufficient evidence.

THE WARNING

144.

As part of his sex education at home, a single mother we know warned her son not to put his hand or any other part of his body or its appendages in, on or around the crotch area of a girl, because in there were very sharp teeth that could do him grievous bodily harm. This put the fear of God in this boy, so he grew up studiously avoiding any such contact. He eventually became a dentist, and in due course he met a very nice and comely young lady who was puzzled by his lack of initiative in making a pass at her. Being the communicative type she sat him down and inquired just why he had been exhibiting indifference to pursuing an intimate relationship with her, all the while hinting that she would not be inclined to reject any such advances. Well, she broke him down, and he told her about his mother's warning. She advised him that she certainly didn't have any teeth in her vulva. He was still not convinced, so she pulled down her panties, spread her legs and told him to take a good close look for himself. Well, he did that, and in fact spread her nether lips apart and made a close visual examination, saying. "With gums like that, no wonder you have no teeth."

THE MYTH

145.

A bunch of the guys are having a few brews one evening at their favorite watering hole, when in walks a conspicuously large Afro-American chap. The guys start speculating about the dimensions of the caudal appendage with which the black guy might be endowed, and references is made to the fact that the the size of black guys' hoo-hoos vis a vis those of the white guys' organs is only a myth. They decide to explore the validity of this rumour by asking the black guy how long his hoo-hoo is. He says, "Three inches." They are amazed and interrogate him further, inquiring how he measures it to get that figure. He replies, "Fum de flo'."

MEDICAL ADVICE

146.

The scene: a doctor's office. A upper middle-aged couple are discussing the wife's recent annual physical. In answer to the doctor's inquiry, the woman discloses that she has sex once a month. The doctor says, "For your well-being you should do it eight times a month." Her husband says, "You can put me down for two."

PESKY PESTS

147.

Picture, if you will…a doctor's office. The physician is examining a young lady who is complaining about a persistent itch in the area of her crotch. The doctor determines that the nether parts of his patient is infested with crab lice. She asks him what the problem is, and he says, very diplomatically, "Young lady, I'm afraid your watergate is bugged."

QUITE NUTTY

148.

Picture, if you will…a confectionary store. A man is looking over a fine display of miscellaneous nuts. He asks the proprietor, "How much are your walnuts?" "$12.95 a pound." "Your pecans?" "$11.95 a pound." "Your cashews?" "$14.95 a pound." "Your pistachios?" "Also $14.95 a pound." The putative customer looks at the store owner very closely and says, "I'll bet that dimple in your chin is actually your belly button. It must be, your nuts are so high!"

THE NEW LAWYER

149.

A brand new lawyer, fresh from the swearing-in ceremony is on the side of the highway hitchhiking. Along comes this beautifully well-rounded and rather comely female motorist in a sleek convertible. She stops and offers him a ride. He hops in, very impressed by his great good fortune in connecting with such a beautiful girl. A few minutes later he starts chuckling, and his driver asks him why, to which he replies, "It's amazing; here I've been an attorney for less than an hour and I'm already thinking about screwing someone!"

WHATEVER

150.

Gentleman to foxy lady: "If I didn't have all this money, would you still love me?" "Yes," she replies, "but I'd miss you."

AN EVENING AT HOME

151.

Picture, if you will...a married couple at home watching T-V. The family dog starts humping the wife's leg, so she says, "Dear, this is terrible; what should I do?" "Do what you always do, my dear; tell him you've got a headache!"

THE FLIGHT ENGINEER

152.

Recently in a popular singles bar in Coconut Grove a a Delta Airlines Flight Engineer was overheard talking to a sweet young thing on the stool adjacent to the one he was occupying. She inquires, "What is it that you do when you are not doing this sort of thing?" He replies, "I'm with Delta Airlines; I'm the romantic adviser to the Captain." "What do you mean, romantic adviser?" she asks. "Well, whenever I venture to suggest any course of action for him to take, he always says, 'If I want any f—n advice from you I'll ask for it.'"

THE COW TOWN

153.

Picture, if you will...a saloon in an old Western town on the edge of the desert in S. California; a cowpoke has just exited the premises. He comes roaring back in twenty seconds later, face red with anger, and hollers, "Okay! Consarn it, who's the no account son of a bitch who painted my horse's testicles yellow?" At this, a giant of a fellow, about six foot six, 285 lbs., gets up from his bar stool and says, "I did; what d'ya want to do about it?" The other, intimidated by the size and shape of the speaker, says rather meekly, "I just wanted you to know that the first coat is dry."

HISTORICAL FACT

154.

The question arises, "What was the first Jewish settlement in the New World?" Answer (After exhaustive research): "50 cents on a dollar."

MAGIC

155.

A man who lives on my street is said to have THE MIDAS TOUCH: everything he touches turns into a muffler.

THE GOOD WORD

156.

The Bible tells us that skin is more elastic than rubber, the reference being the time that Ezekiel tied his ass to a tree and walked 20 miles to do battle.

NO PROBLEM

157.

This is the story of the claustrophobic homosexual: He had no trouble coming out of the closet.

THE CONFESSION

158.

"Bless me, Father, for I have sinned; I traded my wife for a case of whiskey." To which the priest replies, "God will forgive you my son if you want her back again." "Ah, that I do, Father; I'm that thirsty again."

A PARAGON?

159.

One man says, "My son hasn't had a drop of liquor or touched a woman in almost three years!" "You must be very proud of him," says his friend. "I am; and when he gets paroled next month, I'm gonna throw him a big party."

UGLY

160.

She's so ugly she makes her own yogurt...she pours a glass of milk and stares at it!

BIRTH CONTROL

161.

The only method of birth control permitted in Ireland is not a pill. It's a little guy named O'Shaughnesy. You hang him on the bedpost, and every 5 minutes he hollers, "Don't do that!"

MARRIAGE

162.

"I never should have gotten married; she hates me when I'm drunk, and when I'm sober I can't stand her!"

PROBATE

163.

O'Brien's widow was heard to say, "It's taking so long to settle the estate that sometimes I wish he hadn't died!"

GET THE OWNER

164.

A deucedly attractive woman goes up to the bar in a small town pub. She gestures alluringly to the bartender who comes over with great promptitude. When he arrives she seductively signals to bring his face close to hers. When he does so, she begins to gently caress his beard which is full and bushy. "Are you the owner?" she asks, stroking his face with both hands. "Actually, no," he replies. "Can you get him for me; I have to speak to him?" she asks, running her hands up beyond his beard and into his hair. "I'm afraid I can't," breathes the bartender. "Is there anything I can do?" "Yes, there is; I need you to give him a message," she continues huskily, popping two fingers into his mouth and allowing him to suck them gently. "Tell him that there is no toilet tissue in the ladies' room!"

STATUS REPORTS FROM WWII

165.

SNAFU:	Situation normal, all f—d up!
TARFU:	Things are really f—d up!
FUMTU:	F—d up more than usual!
FUBAR:	F—d up beyond all recognition!
JANFU:	Joint Army/Navy f— up!

A GUEST FOR DINNER

166.

Picture, if you will...a small village in the remotest reaches of New Guinea; the inhabitants are cannibals. It is nearly sundown, and the Chief of the Village emerges from the surrounding jungle, crosses the clearing and enters his hut, where he is met by his wife, who says, "George, thank heaven you are home early; hurry up and wash up. We're having Mother for dinner!" George replies, "Dammit, Grace, you know I don't like your mother!" To which Grace replies, "All right then, George, just eat the noodles."

CHAMPAGNE OR BEER?

167.

Picture, if you will...a distinguished elderly gentleman in an elegant cocktail lounge in the company of a dazzlingly gorgeous young blonde. He asks her if she would prefer champagne or beer. She replies, "When I drink champagne, I visualize myself lying nude on the beach at Acapulco, the moon shimmering with a brilliant radiance on the gentle breaking waves, causing an iridescent halo of magnificent colors, when suddenly a gorgeous adonis strides out of the surf to my side, he then drops to his knees and kisses me with all the exquisite tenderness of a zephyr-light breeze billowing through a field of ripe golden wheat. He then caresses my body with his velvet soft hands until I explode with the psychedelic ecstasy of the Aurora Borealis, but when I drink beer, I FART!"

FOR THE DOCTORS

168.

The U/M medical school gives its graduates a batch of ten-year-old magazines, so their patients won't think they are new in the practice.

THE CLAN

169.

How do you tell to what clan a Scotsman belongs? Well, you can't always tell, but if you lift his kilt and it's a quarter-pounder, he's a McDonald.

THE NEWLYWEDS

170.

Bride to new husband, "Okay, you'll wear the pants in this household, but I'll retain the rights to the zipper."

THE PATIENT

171.

New patient walks into doctor's office. He asks, "What do you charge for an office visit?" Dr. says, "$50 for the first visit, and $10 for subsequent visits." Patient says, "Well, here I am again."

THE BANK ROBBERY

172.

The FBI is investigating a bank robbery on Miami Beach. A witness is being interrogated. He says that the perpetrator was an elephant. The FBI guy says, "Was it an African or Indian elephant; the African elephant has very large ears, and the Indian elephant has smaller ears." "Gee," says the witness, "I can't really say; he was wearing a stocking mask."

THE DREAMER

173.

I have a friend that says that he likes wet dreams better than sexual intercourse. Says he meets a better class of women in his dreams.

THE NUNS

174.

Picture, if you will…two nuns in New Orleans who get caught in the rain and duck into a cat house for shelter. They strike up a conversation with the girls who work in the establishment, because they are very curious about that type of activity that takes place there. One nun says, "Well, ladies, what do you get from the men you have sex with?" "Anywhere from $50 to $100 usually." One nun whispers to the other, "Oh! that Father Reilly…him and his Hershey Bars!"

TELLING TIME

175.

Picture, if you will…a nudist camp. A new member has just been admitted. It seems that he has a perpetual erection which makes for a good deal of grumbling among the other nudists. They tell him that they don't appreciate his walking around in that tumescent state, and he explains, "Oh, don't get upset, this is the way I tell time; sort of like a sundial; see, it's 11:10." One of the others says, "No, it isn't; it's 11:30." "Oh, damn," says the erectile one, masturbating frantically, "it's running slow again!"

NO ENEMIES

176.

A preacher is giving a sermon the thrust of which is what a wonderful world it would be if no one had enemies, only friends. He says that unfortunately everyone seems to have enemies. "In fact," he says, "Is there a person present who can honestly say that he has no enemies." A hand is raised in the middle of the group; it is 94-year-old Harold Johnson, who says, "Me, Father." The preacher says, "To what do you attribute this unique situation, Brother Johnson?" To this the other replies, "I outlived the bastards!"

CROSS BETWEEN

177.

What do you get when you cross a rooster with an owl? Answer: A cock that stays up all night.

WHICH ONE?

178.

Which of the following doesn't fit?
    AIDS
    Herpes
    Gonorrhea
    Condo on Brickell

Answer: Gonorrhea…that's the only one you can get rid of.

THE FRIENDLY NEIGHBOR

179.

A young man has just parked his car in the lot adjacent to the apartment house in which he resides. He looks up and sees a beauteous young lady dressed in something filmy who is waving her arms frantically. He finally concludes that she is waving at him, whereupon she drops a crumpled piece of paper indicating that it is for him. He retrieves it, smoothes it out and reads it. "Please come up to apartment 3-G immediately. It's important that I meet you." He is intrigued and pleased; she is a foxy looking lady. He proceeds to the apartment in question and knocks. She answers the door promptly; she is dressed in a conspicuously sexy peignoir…and nothing else. Her body is luscious. She says, seductively, "Come in and take off your clothes." He is pleased to comply with her request in this regard and is quite flabbergasted as to what is taking place. When he is nude, she takes his hand and leads him over to a couch. She says, "You have a marvelous body, and your penis is beautiful; may I fondle it?" He embraces her suggestion with enthusiasm. Whereupon, she starts stroking it and cupping his balls while making sweet cooing sounds. He is ecstatic, when suddenly she grabs his testicles while twisting them sharply, bringing him to his knees in agony. She says, "Now, I want you to promise me you will never park your car in space 306 again!"

THE ULTIMATE REJECTION

180.

This is when you are masturbating, and your hand goes to sleep.

HIGHER EDUCATION

181.

There was a clique of American girls going to school in Paree. One day the father of one of these girls gets a letter from her in which she asks him to send her fifty dollars so she can buy a bicycle. She says, "All the girls are getting bikes, Daddy." He sends her the fifty, but by the time the money arrives the fad has changed, and all the girls are buying monkeys, so she uses the bike money to buy a monkey. In a subsequent letter to her father, the girl writes, "All the hair is falling off my monkey, and I don't know what to do?!" The father cables back immediately, "For God's sakes, Sweetheart, get rid of that bicycle!"

THE NUDE IN THE CAKE

182.

The other night I attended a bachelor party…the guy was going to be married the next day. It was somewhat typical. A nude girl arose from the middle of this big cake, and she was so ugly that we gang-dressed her!

THE PEEPING TOM

183.

We have a peeping tom in our neighborhood, and one night he was looking through the window into this girl's bedroom where she stood absolutely nude. Well…she was so ugly that he broke into her house and pulled down the shade.

HOME MOVIES

184.

There's a family down the block from our house and they are heavy into home movies with a video camera, of course. They take some footage of the family members every month. Well…the daughter is so ugly that they have hired an actress to play her part.

THE DENTISTE

185.

My Uncle Hank goes to a lady dentist, because, he says, that's the only woman he's ever met who tells him to open his mouth, not shut it.

A BAD DREAM

186.

Picture, if you will…a doctor's office; the doctor is questioning a man regarding his reason for being there. The patient says, "Doc, I have this recurring dream; several beautiful naked young girls keep forcing themselves upon me, and I keep fending them off with my hands." "that's interesting all right, but what is it that I can do for you that you think will help?" "Well," says the man, "the solution is pretty obvious, don't you think; I want you to break my arms."

THE SOLUTION

187.

Picture, if you will…a psychiatrist's office. A beautiful, sensuous, voluptuous, exotic young lady is telling the doctor, "Doctor, every time I go out with a young man I wind up saying 'Yes', and then afterward I feel guilty and I'm depressed all day long." "Ah" says the doctor, "You want me to help you strengthen your will power, is that it?" "No", she replies, "I want you to help me weaken my conscience."

NO COMPARISON

188.

A little boy and a little girl who lives next door are out playing in the back yard. The little boy pulls his shorts down thereby exposing his little hoo-hoo. He says, "Here's something I bet you don't have." At this the little girl pulls down her panties, and, pointing to her little pussy, says, "That's okay; Mommie says that with one of these I can get all of those I want."

THE COLLECTION

189.

In St. Ignatius Catholic Church the principal collection has just been consolidated at the altar, and the Parish Priest, Father O'Brien, notices that someone has contributed a nice crisp fifty dollar bill. He acknowledges this miracle of human compassion and says, "Whoever made this donation can choose three hymns this morning." With this said, a swishy young man stands up and, using his finger as a pointer, says, "I'll take HIM, and HIM and HIM."

UP FRONT

190.

The question arises: Why do so many women fake orgasms? The somewhat obvious answer is: Because so many men fake foreplay.

THE ROOKIE ITALIAN PARATROOPERS

191.

This is a story about two Southern Italian boys about 20 years old. One of them is called Big Tony, because he is big, hearty, animated, arm-waving (wave your arms) and talks loudly to everybody. (Loudly say: "Hey, Pietro, come sta?" "Hey, Maria, agimme a kiss.")

The other boy, Luigi, is quiet; just as tall, but slim, a bit shy, not too demonstrative. (Hunch your shoulders and look a little furtive.) But still a very nice young man.

It so happens that the economy in Southern Italy is very bad...as it often is...so a-Big-a Tony talks quiet Luigi into doing something positive about this for themselves...by joining the Italian paratroops. (Now animatedly, with arms gesturing.) "Come on-a-Luigi, you a-gonna get three a-big-a pasta meals a day; you a-gonna get all new clothes; you a-gonna be a big-a shot. No more joost-a poor Italian farm-a boy. You a-gonna travel in a-big-a air-a-plane (soar with arms) to famous-a places. You a-gonna float like-a da bee-you-ti-ful butterfly (here flap arms) and land-a like-a pussy-cat (little jump)."

So Big-a Tony and quiet Luigi sign up for the Italian paratroops, get their new uniforms, three big pasta meals a day and go right straight through the exciting and very rigorous training like paratroops everywhere.

Well, Big-a Tony loves every minute of it, and quiet Luigi hangs right in there with him. But then graduation day finally rolls around when they have to get aboard "a-big-a air-a-plane" and make their very first real parachute jump from about 5,000 feet in the air; not the tower-on-the-ground safety-rope jump routine.

As expected, Big-a-Tony is eager, but quiet Luigi is far from it. As one after the other stands up in the plane when the jump light comes on and bails out the door, quiet Luigi confides to BIG-a-Tony that he is scared out of his wits...*really* scared. Big-a-Tony says, "Luigi, a-what-za matter? It's-a easy (Extend arms in confidence) You joost hook-a up ...step-a out, and thees-a cord she-za pull-a da chute open *for you*! (Arms again, as if pulling the rip cord). Come on; just watch a-Big-a-Tony." With that, it's Tony's turn; he hooks up and jumps out the door in a-big-a swan dive (Demo the swan dive). His chute pops open, and he loves the whole effect...then looks back up at the plane for Luigi. Just then he sees the jump master *shove* Luigi out the door, all hunched up, frightened. He tumbles; his chute opens but the shroud lines get all tangled up, and he starts falling like a rock with the chute dragging behind, only slightly open.

Big-a-Tony sees this immediately. He knows that Luigi is in grave peril, so Big-a-Tony pulls on his shroud lines to position himself right under Luigi's fall-path. He hollers up, "Hey, Luigi, don't-a you worry, your friend a-big-a Tony is right here. (Hands to mouth hollering up) Ah-mmma gonna catch-a you in-a- my arms." (WHAP!) He clamps his arms around the falling Luigi in a big bear hug...and they begin floating gently downward toward the ground below. Luigi is totally overwhelmed by this magnificent feat and the fact that he has been snatched from the jaws of certain death. He breaks out into sobs and says, "Tony, Tony, my dear friend, you have saved my life!"

At this, Tony is very touched and replies, "Luigi, Luigi, don't-a you cry. After all, what are friends for?!" (Open arms full width.)

<u>OUT OF SPANISH FLY</u>

192.

Picture, if you will...a small pharmacy. A man walks in and up to the service window and says, "I'd like to buy some Spanish Fly." The pharmacist says, "We are all out of Spanish Fly; all we have is Jewish Fly." "What's Jewish Fly?", the man inquires. "Well, says the pharmacist, "You give it to a girl and almost immediately she wants to go shopping."

<u>THE G Y N AND THE PIZZA DELIVERY BOY</u>

193.

Q. How are a gynecologist and a pizza delivery boy alike?
A. They can both smell it, but they can't eat it.

EXCITEMENT!

194.

Picture, if you will...a schoolroom in an elementary school, fourth grade. The teacher says, "All right children, today we're going to play a little game; I'm going to call on several of you, and when I call your name, you come up to the blackboard and write down one word that signifies 'excitement'. Johnny, you're first."

Johnny comes up and neatly prints the word "Skydiver", and is complimented by the teacher. Next she calls on Wilfred, who writes the word "Ambulance". This, too, gets the approval of the teacher.

The next student to get the nod is Emily who comes to the board and instead of a word just puts a dot and returns to her seat. The teacher says, "Emily, a dot is not a word." And Emily says, "Miss Russell, that's not a dot, it's a period. This morning at breakfast my sister told us that she has missed two of them, and boy! talk about excitement!"

A REAL TREAT

195.

Picture, if you will...an elegantly furnished apartment inhabited by two compatible gay fellows. The day before one of them had taken a dozen condoms and filled them with a variety of juices and placed them in the freezer. Today, now they're frozen, and his longtime companion finds them and claps his hands together joyfully and says, "Oh, you dear boy, my favorite treat, 'Cocksicles'!"

THE WELCOME STRANGER

196.

Picture, if you will...a bar that caters to sexual deviants. A stranger comes in, and this guy looks really straight, so the bartender inquires, on behalf of all those present, "Hi, stranger, where do you hail from?" The newcomer says, "I'm from Maine." The bartender inquires further, "What do you do up there in Maine?" The man says, "I'm a taxidermist." "Oh, really; well, what does a taxidermist do?" And the man replies, "I mount animals; that 's what I do." With this, the bartender says to the crowd, "It's okay, guys, he's one of us."

THE TRAVELLER

197.

Picture, if you will...a storefront travel agency. A client is speaking to one of the agents, a close friend of his, "I want you to arrange a trip for me, Jack. In the past three years you've sent me to Bali, Turkey and Russia. This time I want it closer to home; the last three times my wife got pregnant."

THE ORIGIN OF THE SPECIES

198.

Picture, if you will...a doctor's office. A lady is there having her annual check-up. She tells the doctor that she has a question she feels he might be able to answer for her, to wit: "Doctor, tell me, is there anything wrong with anal sex?"

The doctor replies, "No, not really; do you enjoy it?"

"Yes, I do," says the patient/examinee.

"Well," says the doctor, "it's just a matter of keeping the working parts clean, and, of course, you want to avoid getting pregnant!"

"Pregnant? Can I get pregnant by having anal sex?," asks the lady.

"Of course you can!" the doctor says, "Where do you think lawyers come from?"

ELDERLY INFIDELITY

199.

Picture, if you will...an upper floor of a high-rise apartment building. An elderly woman comes home unexpectedly to find her 80-year-old husband in bed boffing a 23-year-old chick. The offended woman thereupon throws her husband out the window, and the chick says, "Why did you do that? He'll be killed!"

To this the woman replies, "I don't know; I figure that if he can f— at his age, he can probably fly too!"

A SPORTING PROPOSITION

200.

Picture, if you will...a couple out on a blind date. He wines and dines her, and then says, "How'd you like to go over to my place for some friendly sexual intercourse?"

"Fine with me; I'm a good sport!"

So, they do that, and a month later he gets a call from her; she says, "Well, that night we spent together last month was a little reckless of us; I'm pregnant! And I'm going to kill myself!!"

To this he says, "Boy, you *ARE* a good sport!"

THE LOST DOG

201.

From the bulletin board: "LOST DOG. Three legs, blind in left eye, right ear missing, tail broken, accidentally neutered; answers to name, 'LUCKY'"

FOREPLAY

202.

In the Irish household, "Brace yerself, Bridget!"

If your bride is a J.A.P: 30 minutes of begging.
In the WASP household: Drying the dishes.
In the ghetto: "If you scream, I'll kill you!"

MOVING OUT

203.

Picture, if you will…a man in his office; it's ten-thirty A.M.; he gets a phone call from his live-in girl friend who announces that she is leaving him. He is dead set against that moving out concept, so he says, "I'll be right home; we can discuss this."

So he goes home, and he finds that she has already packed and is dressed to go out, so he asks what this is all about, and she says, "I'm moving out, because my girl friend says you are a pedophile."

To this he says, "My, my, that's a pretty big word for a 9-year old!"

THE DAY OFF

204.

Picture, if you will…a classroom; it's Thursday; the teacher says that she is going to throw out a famous saying and wants someone to tell her who said it. She says, "The student who gives the right answer can take the next day, Friday, off from school. The first one is: 'Who said that he was for separate but equal facilities for the colored and the whites?" Little Shandra Jo raises her hand and says "That was Malcolm X said that." The teacher says that that was right and tells the little girl that she doesn't have to come to school the next day.

Little Shandra Jo says "Thank you, teacher, but I like school, so I don't want to take the day off."

The next question was, "Who said 'I have a dream'…" And Mandy Lou correctly says that it was Martin Luther King, Jr. at the Lincoln Memorial in Washington who said that. Again the teacher says she can have Friday off, but Mandy Lou, like Shandra Jo, says she really likes school and would not take the day off.

At this point a voice from the back of the classroom mutters, "Stupid ni—ers!" to which the teacher says "Who said that?" And a voice says, "Mark Furman, teacher; see you Monday!"

WHO SAID THAT?

205.

(This you can pull on a friend or person of your choosing):

Q. Who said, "Give me liberty, or give me death!"?
A. (From your victim), "Patrick Henry."

Q. Who said, "Ask not what your country can do for you; ask what you can do for your country."

A. (From your victim): "JFK".

Q. Who said, "What the f— was that?" Your victim says, "I don't know; you tell me."

A. "The Lord Mayor of Hiroshima!"

THE BLESSED EVENT

206.

Picture, if you will…a delivery room in a hospital; a hooker has just given birth, and the nurse tells the mother that she has given birth to a most unusual baby boy; he has the kinky hair of a negro, the slanted eyes of an oriental and the white skin of a Caucasian. The doctor then slaps the baby's little behind, and he let's out a splendid cry. The mother crosses herself and says, "Thank God he didn't bark!"

THE LAWS OF PHYSICS

207.

Q. When a bug hits the windshield, what is the last thing to go through his mind?

A. His ass!

PRESIDENTIAL SUCCESSION

208.

When it was announced two years ago that Tipper Gore had gone into the Betty Ford place to lose weight, actually she had moved out on Al suggesting that she wanted a divorce. He prevailed upon her to visit a marriage counselor and promised that he also would do that, because he really wanted to save the marriage, realizing that she was a lot better than he deserved.

She goes first and the counselor elicits from her just why she wants a divorce. She says, "Al has changed; he's acquired a bad habit that disgusts me; he's always picking his nose, and he used to be such a gentleman; not only that, our sex life has deteriorated: he knows that I get the most pleasure during intercourse when I am on top, but he now refuses to indulge my preference in that regard; that's why I want a divorce!"

Next day the counselor sees Al and reveals to him what Tipper had said about his nose and the sex, and Al says, "I was just trying to follow what Clinton told me a couple of months ago; that's all; Bill said, 'Al, if you want to be President, just keep your nose clean and don't f—k up!'"

A POIGNANT MOMENT

209.

Picture, if you will…a funeral parlor; they have a recently deceased gentleman in a casket, and they find that they cannot close the lid, because the deceased has a tremendous hoo-hoo in a state of substantially vertical erection that prevents this. They call the widow, and she suggests very respectfully that they cut if off and shove it up his a—. They do this, and the widow comes over to the funeral parlor later in the day to review the remains, and, looking very closely, she sees that there is a tear running down the cheek of the deceased. She bends down and whispers in his ear, "See…I told you it hurt!"

A WISE CHOICE

210.

Picture, if you will…two little colored kids who have just received their allowance for the week. One says to the other, "Whut you gone do wit yo allowance, Bro?"

The other replies, "Ahz gone to de drug sto' an' buy me some tampax, das whut."

"Whuffo you gone buy dat fo'?"

"Well, ah read in a magazine dat if you haz tampax, yo kin go swimmin'. water skiin', horseback ridin'…an' de like!"

THE TOES KNOWS

211.

Picture, if you will…a very pretty twentyish young lady talking to her doctor; her annual physical is under way, and the doctor asks her if there is anything particular that is bothering her.

She says, "Well, there is one thing, doctor, whenever my boy friend kisses me I get this this really heavy itch between my toes!"

"Hmmmm," says the doctor, "which toes are involved?"

The patient replies, "My two big toes!

FOOD FOR THOUGHT

212.

Q. What's the difference between a J.A.P. and a bowl of spaghetti?
A. When you eat a bowl of spaghetti, it moves.

THE LOGICAL QUESTION

213.

If God did not want man to eat it, why did he make it look like a taco?

THE CHANGE

214.

Over at the nunnery they have been joined by a nun who has gone through a sex change. Her name? Transister Madeline.

THE BUSINESSMEN'S IDEA OF TROUBLE

215.

Picture, if you will…two Jewish businessmen meeting after not having talked in several months. One says, I hef lifd tru a Somma I tawt I'd neva see. June vuz a disastuh; neva hef I seen a June like det, and July vuz even verse; I vent right into de cellah!" The other replies, "Vy are you comink at me wid dese piddling mattuhs? You vanta heah real trobble? I got it! My only son comes to me and says he's a homosexual and he's gonna move in to our house wid his lovuh. Vut could be verse den dat?" "I'll tal you, says the first, 'August'."

DINNER INVITATION

216.

Remember, in the Cuban community in Miami, when you are invited to dinner at 7:30, it doesn't mean 7:29 and it doesn't mean 7:31; it means 10:30!

A VARIATION OF STYLE

217.

Picture, if you will…two guys rapping. One says to the other, "Do you and your wife ever do it dog style?"

His buddy replies, "It's more like trick-dog style; whenever I make a move toward her these days, she rolls over and plays dead!"

A CHARITABLE GESTURE

218.

Picture, if you will…the headquarters for the Red Cross annual clothing drive; it is a storefront operation. I nice little old lady comes in with a package wrapped in brown paper and tied with white grocery-store string; she says, quite proudly, "I'd like to donate these to the clothing drive; they're men's pajamas; I made them myself!"

"Well, now, Madam; that's very nice of you to take the trouble to do all that cutting and sewing; let's take a look at them, okay?", says the man behind the counter. With this he unties and unwraps the package and holds up the pajamas for a looksee. He notices that there is no fly in the trousers and calls that to her attention. To which she replies, slightly flustered and defensive, "Well, couldn't you give them to a bachelor?!!

WHAT? WHY? WHO?

219.

What's the difference between a dog and a fox? About 5 drinks.

What's the best thing to come out of a hoo-hoo? The wrinkles.

Why are Jewish men circumcised? Jewish women don't go for anything unless it's 20% off.

Why did God create women? Because sheep can't cook.

What resulted from the union between the black and the Japanese lady? A guy who has an uncontrollable urge on December 7th to attack Pearl Bailey.

What do you get when you cross a Mexican and an Italian? A guy who makes you an offer you can't understand.

Who are the two most famous black women of all time" Aunt Jemima and Mother F—r.

What they say about virginity: A big issue about a little tissue.

What do you call the JAP's water bed? The Dead Sea.

What's the difference between the Irish Wedding and an Irish funeral? One less drunk.

How do you say F you in Hollywood? "Trust me!"

What do you get when you cross a black with a ground hog? Six more weeks of basketball.

The name of the new black French Restaurant: "Chez What?"

What did Lincoln say when he recovered from a 5-day drunk? "I freed who?"

What's the JAP's idea of natural childbirth? Absolutely no make-up.

Why do JAP's close their eyes while making love? So they can pretend that they're shopping.

Why are passed gases malodorous? So that deaf people can enjoy them too.

Why do women rub their eyes when they get out of bed in the morning? Because they don't have balls to scratch.

Is it better to be born black or gay? Black, because you don't have to tell your parents.

How is sex like a bridge game? You don't need a partner if you have a good hand.

What's organic dental floss? Pubic hair.

What's the JAP's idea of perfect sex? Simultaneous headaches.

What's the quintessential personification of machismo? Jogging home from your own vasectomy.

The new gay bar in town: "Boys-R-Us."

Why don't black women make good nuns? Because they can't say "Superior" after "Mother".

What's a Greek gentleman? A Greek guy who takes a girl out three times before propositioning her brother.

FROM SHOES TO SWEATERS
(This is a visual story)

220.

Picture, if you will…an average horny guy selling shoes to ladies in Macy's. His boss has received several complaints from some good customers to the effect that he has been looking up their skirts while engaged in fitting them. The store does not want to fire him, because he is such a hot shot salesman, so they transfer him over to women's sweaters. Well, this conspicuously curvaceous lady comes to the ladies' sweater department, and she is immediately approached by the salesman of this story who induces her to slip on a very nice cashmere sweater. He looks at her admiringly and taking a piece of chalk in hand draws rectangles over each of her breasts on the sweater saying, "This is how it would look if we were to add pockets to this lovely cashmere sweater." To this the customer says, "I don't want pockets; I like it just the way it is!" "Well," says the salesman, "then we'll just take those pockets off!" (rubbing his hands up and down on her breasts to erase the chalk marks.)

THE FRENCH FIGHTER PILOT

221.

Pierre, ze famous French fighter pilot, a triple ace (fifteen victories in the air over Messerschmits and Focke-Wolfes), is in the Eisenhower Suite of the Henry the Fifth Hotel in Paris, having just arrived from the front for a little rest and rehabilitation. He is in bed with this most elegantly attractive young nude girl. He takes a bottle of Dom Perignon champagne and pours it all over her shoulders and then devours her shoulders with passionate kisses. She says, "Oh, Pierre, why do you do zat wiz ze champagne?" And he replies, "Your shoulders, zey are so white, ze deserve ze best champagne; Pierre always takes ze champagne wiz ze white meat!" Next, Pierre pours some Vin Rose all over the breasts of the girl and kisses most passionately the lovely pick nipples, taking them into his mouth and running his tongue back and forth across their erect perfection. She says, "Oh, Pierre, why do you pour ze vin rose all over my breasts like zat?" To which Pierre says, "Your nipples are so perfectly pink, I use ze vin rose; Pierre always takes vin rose with ze pink meat!" The lovemakinh progresses, and Pierre takes a bottle of the best Courvoisier cognac, pours it on her pussy and then he sets it on fire with a solid gold Dunhill lighter and starts to go down on her. She shrieks, "Pierre, why do you set my pussy on fire like zat?" And Pierre replies, "Pierre is ze greatest fighter pilot in all of France, and when Pierre goes down he goes down in flames!"

THE CAB DRIVER

222.

A businessman has just boarded a taxicab at the Boston International Airport; he is in town to attend a convention of others in his irrelevant line of work. The cabbie says, "Where can I take you, mister?" "Well," says the passenger, "first I'd like to get scrod!" To this the cabbie says, "I admit that I have had this request many times during my years as a cabbie here in Boston, but this is the first time I have ever heard it phrased in the pluperfect subjunctive!"

JELLO

223.

What can Jello do that you can't do? Ans. Come in six delicious flavors.

INTERACTION

224.

This couple meets at a cocktail party, and they make it quite clear to each other that mutual physical activity is likely to ensue. In fact the guy intimates almost in so many words that he is going to make love to her with such enthusiasm and competence it will make all her previous bouts of this nature pale by comparison. Well, it eventuates that they do wind up in bed together and he is going at it, so to speak, when she pulls a feather out of the pillow and starts flicking it against his forehead. He pauses and says, "What are you doing with that feather, Darling?" To this, she replies, "Well, relatively speaking, my dear, I'm beating your brains out."

SHIPWRECKED

225.

Out in the middle of nowhere in the Pacific Ocean a luxury yacht goes down. Six girls and one guy grab some of the floating wreckage and make their way to what turns out to be a deserted island. After awhile the six girls have a meeting and decide that they are going to want to have sex but have to be fair to the guy, so they inform him that it will be his pleasant duty to have one night a week with each girl. He agrees to this on the condition that they give him Sundays off. Well, this works out fine, and everything is going smoothly for several months. Finally, one day they see a speck on the horizon that eventually they discern to be another man who is hanging onto a piece of wreckage of some sort. The seven of them already are developing plans for some sexual diversion as he gets closer. When the man finally staggers out of the surf, hugs the guy and says, with a slight lisp, "Oh boy, Sweetycakes, am I ever glad to see you; it's just been so simply awful out there." With this, the guy says, "Well, there go my Sundays!"

DEATH IN THE FAMILY

226.

Picture, if you will...a Catholic church in a semi-rural parish in Ireland. A wealthy farmer/landowner accosts the priest and says, "Father, it is a great tragedy we have been sufferin'; me dog died; he'd been with us fifteen years, a treasured member of me family. I was just wonderin' if you could says a few words for him at mass this comin' Sunday?" "Oh," says the priest, "that is a great tragedy, and I sympathize wi' ye', I do, but sadly the Catholic Church does not hold services for the animals, but there is a sorta new church down the road a few miles, and lord knows what they're up to; perhaps they might have a service for your dear departed pet." "Oh, thank you, Father," he says, "and say, Father, do you think a payment to them of twenty thousand pounds would be enough in showin' my appreciation for that?" "Oh," says the priest, "why din't ya tell me that the dog was a Catholic?"

THE HANDYMAN

227.

Picture, if you will...a construction site in Dublin. A man approaches the foreman and says, "I'm here in answer to yer ad fer a handyman." "Oh, good," says the foreman, "Glad I am ta have ya; I kin put ya right ta work over here with some electrical stuff." The other says, "I know nuthin' a'tall a' tall about electrical stuff." "That's okay, I need some tile ta be laid over here in the carner." "I know nothin' a'tall about the layin' a tile." "Not to worry, then, we've got some carpentry we gotta take care of over here." "I know nothin' a'tall about carpentry," says the job seeker. "Well," says the foreman, "kin ya tell me whut makes ya such a handyman?" The answer comes, "I live right around the carner!"

THE TRAIN TO DUBLIN

228.

Picture, if you will...the train from from Killarney to Dublin. This man comes from one car to the next and asks rather loudly, "Is there a Catholic priest among us?" He gets no answer, so he goes back to his car. A few minutes elapse, and he comes back to the other car and says, "Is there perhaps a Protestant Vicar here?" Getting no reply, he starts back to his car. A man pops up and says, I'm a Baptist Minister, might I be of assistance?" The other replies, "I don't think so...we're lookin' for a corkscrew!"

THE DUCK HUNTERS

229.

Finnegan and Flaherty are givin' ta understand that duck hunting is *THE* thing ta do, so they rent a duck blind and some dogs and hie away to the swamps at 6:00 the next marnin'. Well, they stay in that miserable, wet, nasty, uncomfortable duck blind all the day long with no ducks bagged. Flaherty says, "Finnegan, we bin here fer twelve hours and have'n got a single duck; we're doin' sumthin' wrong, I'm thinkin'." "Yeah," says Finnegan, I think I know whut it is thet we're doin' wrong: we're not throwin" the dogs high enough!"

SOMETHING TO WORRY ABOUT

230.

One Sunday we had a visiting preacher in our church who was invited to deliver the sermon. Well, every time he wanted to make a point he slammed either his right or left hand down forcefully on the pulpit. A little girl was there with her parents, and about halfway through the sermon she whispered to her Dad, "Daddy, whatever shall we do if he gets out of there?"

231.

What's the height of conceit? Shouting your own name while having an orgasm.

She said I was a lousy lay. How can she make a judgment like that after two minutes?

What d'ya get when you cross an oversexed girl with an elephant? You get a two-ton nympho who does it for peanuts…and never forgets you.

HAPPY PARENTS

232.

Happy are the parents who have no children.

HEREDITY

233.

Heredity means that if your parents didn't have any children, the odds are that you won't either.

RECOVERY ROOM

234.

Patient: Is it okay for me to read magazines?
Doctor: Sure; but don't read any serials.

THE BEQUEST

235.

My brother-in-law gave all his money to sick horses. He didn't know they were sick when he bet on them.

THE MOTHER-IN-LAW

236.

My cousin Jack's mother-in-law has been staying with them for five years and is a constant source of irritation for him. He decides to take the bull by the horns, so to speak, and lay down the law to his wife, so he says, "We've got to talk; your mother has been living here with us for five years now; don't you think that it is about time for her to move out and get a place of her own?!" His wife is amazed by this and screams, "*My* mother? I thought she was *your* mother!"

THE CELL PHONE

237.

Picture, if you will...the men's locker room at the golf club. A cell phone rings, and one of the men picks it up, and a voice at the other end says, "Hello, darling, I'm down at the jewelers looking at some bracelets, but the one I want is too expensive: $20,000." "That's okay, darling," he says, "I want you to have it, you're worth it." "Oh, thanks darling, that's really sweet of you. Now I'm off to Neiman's to look at the mink coat I've been thinking about." "That's fine, darling," he says; if you like it, buy it." "Oh, you're a dear," she says.
Then he continues, "Oh by the way, as long as you are in the area, go on over to the Mercedes place; I want you to have that new convertible with the V-12 engine; I think it's about $132,500; you'll look really good in it." She effusively thanks him and says, "About the new house we've been looking at on the lake that's been listed at $925,000; I heard that they might take $875,000 if we get a firm offer into the realtor by 4:00 this afternoon. If you agree, I can use that power-of-attorney you gave me and tie it right up." "Great," he says, "go make that offer to the realtor; I know he'll honor the power-of-attorney; good thinking, dear." "All right, Sweetie, get with it...good-bye." "Good bye." Then he pushes the "end" button on the instrument, looks around and says, "Hey you guys, anyone know whose cell phone this is?"

THE PARROT

238.

This lady acquires a parrot which has been guaranteed to speak when spoken to. Next day she says to the bird, "Nice day, isn't it?" The parrot says, "Nice day, isn't it?" The next day she says, "Hello, Beautiful." and the parrot says, "Hello, Beautiful." It eventually eventuates that the parrot daily initiates the colloquy with its mistress with innocuous greetings, remarks, questions and the like, and one day he says to the lady, "How's your hole?" To this the lady retorts rather sharply, "Shut up!" The bird rejoins, "Mine, too; must be the salt air!"

THE FORMULA

239.

Picture, if you will…two black guys in the men's room at adjacent urinals. One says to the other, "Mah goodness, that hoo-hoo you got theah am an organ of gran' propo'tions; how you get dat, man?" The other says, "Well, ah has a routine: evah nite ah pours olive on it and strokes it real good, an' as a result it done grown to dis sahz." So they meet again several months later under substantially similar circumstances, and the guy with the big hoo-hoo asks the other, "Well, did ya do mah routine wi' the olive oil on yo hoo-hoo lak ah done said?" "Not zackly; ah din have no olive oil in de house, it's too spensive, so ah done used Crisco, an ah din get no results ay tall." "Well, ah ain't suprizd 'bout dat; evabody knose dat Crisco is shortnin'."

HAIR REMOVER

240.

A lady we know has recently acquired a Schnauser, which is a kind of a dog. She was concerned, because the dog had an excess of hair in his ears, so she went to the pharmacy to get a depilatory. She says to the lady behind the counter, "I need a hair remover." The lady replies, "Well, if you use it on your under arms, you shouldn't wear a tight sweater for a couple of days. If you use it on your legs, you shouldn't wear stockings for a couple of days." "Oh, no," she says, "It's for my Schnauzer." "Okay," says the other, "In that case, don't ride a bike for a couple of days."

THE SONGSTER

241.

Picture, if you will…a gentleman having a dry martini (shaken, not stirred!) in a conspicuously elegant cocktail lounge. A pianist is supplying some sweet sweet background music for the crowd. He plays several old favorites and then the most beautiful melody that the martini quaffer has ever heard. He approaches the pianist and tells him of his overwhelmence and asks him about the song. The pianist says, "This is something I wrote myself, in fact just a few days ago; I'm thinking of finding someone to publish it." The listener says, "Maybe I can help you with that; I've got some connections with song publishers; I'm sure it will be a great hit; what's the name of the song?" The pianist replies, "I call it 'Don't F—k Around With Love'".

PERFECT JUSTICE

242.

Picture, if you will…two gentlemen walking down the street in an urban area; about 20 feet ahead of them is an outrageously attractive girl. One of the men says, "I'd give a hundred bucks to spend a night with that girl." She overhears this remark, looks the man up and down and says, "I'll take you up on that." So they proceed to her apartment and consummate the arrangement.

The next morning as he is preparing to leave, he thanks her and hands her a fifty-dollar bill. She demands the rest of the agreed price, but he declines. She says, "A deal is a deal; I'll sue you for the balance." "Hah!" he says and leaves.

The next day our hero is surprised when served a summons and complaint naming him as a defendant in a lawsuit and requiring his appearance. He hurries to his lawyer's office and explains the details of the case. His lawyer opines "There is no way she can be awarded a judgment on those facts, but it would be interesting to see how the case is presented."

The day of the trial arrives, and after the usual preliminaries, the plaintiff's lawyer addresses the Court as follows: "Your Honor, my client is a young lady who is possessed of a piece of property...a garden spot, surrounded by a profuse growth of shrubbery, which she agreed to rent to the defendant for a specified period of time for the sum of $100. The defendant took occupancy of the property, used it extensively for the purpose for which it had been rented, but upon evacuating the premises he paid her only $50, one-half of the amount agreed upon. The rent was not excessive, since it is restricted property. We request a judgment against the defendant to assure the payment of the balance."

Defendant's attorney is impressed and amused by the way opposing counsel has presented his case. His defense, therefore, is somewhat altered from the way he had originally planned. "Your Honor," he says, my client agrees that the plaintiff has a fine piece of property and that he did rent it for a period of time, and that much pleasure was derived from the occupancy; however, my client found a well on the property, around which he placed stones, sunk a shaft and erected a pump, all labor being personally performed by him. We claim these improvements to the property were sufficient in value to offset the unpaid amount, and that the plaintiff has been adequately compensated for the rental of this property. Accordingly, we ask that judgment not be entered as prayed by plaintiff."

The plaintiff's rebuttal was this, "My client agrees that the defendant did find a well on the property and that he did make the improvements such as described by my opponent. However, had the defendant not known that the well existed, he would not have rented the property. Also, upon evacuating the property, the defendant removed the stones, pulled out the shaft and took the pump with him. And, in so doing, he dragged his equipment through the shrubbery, leaving the hole larger than it was prior to his occupancy, making it easily accessible to members of the public. Accordingly, we renew our request for judgment." And she got it!

<u>FIVE CONSTIPATED MEN MENTIONED IN THE BIBLE</u>

243.

1.   Cain; he wasn't Abel.
2.   Moses; he took two tablets
3.   David; he sat on the throne for 30 years.
4.   Balen; he had trouble with his ass.
5.   Titus; his name speaks for itself.

<u>THE NEW PRIEST</u>

244.

A new priest conducting his first mass was so scared he could hardly even speak. After mass he asked the Monsignor how he had done. He said "Fine," but suggested that next week before mass he might put a little vodka in his water glass to help relax him.

The next Sunday the new priest put vodka in his water glass and really talked up a storm. After mass he again asked the Monsignor how he had done, and the Monsignor said "Fine, but there are few things that should be straightened out, namely:

1.   There are 10 Commandments not 12.
2.   There are 12 disciples not 10.
3.   David slew Goliath; he didn't kick the s—t out of him.
4.   We do not refer to Jesus Christ as 'the late J.C.'
5.   Next Sunday evening there is a taffy-pulling contest at St. Peter's, not a peter-pulling contest at St. Taffy's.
6.   The Holy Trinity are not referred to as 'Big Daddy, Junior and the spook.'"

<u>AIRLINE NOMENCLATURE</u>

245.

Then there is the one about the neophyte airline flight attendant who thout that a tail assembly was a company picnic.

<u>YOU KNOW YOU'RE GROWING OLDER, IF…</u>

246.

1.   Almost everything hurts, and what doesn't hurt doesn't work.
2.   The gleam in your eye is from the sun hitting your bi-focals.
3.   Your little black book contains only names that end in M.D.
4.   You join the health club and then don't go.
5.   You finally reach the top of the ladder, and it's leaning against the wrong wall.
6.   You're still chasing women but can't remember why.

7.   You know all the answers, but nobody asks you the questions.
8.   You sit in a rocking chair but can't make it go.
9.   Your back goes out more than you do.
10. The little gray-haired lady you helped across the street is your wife.
11. You sink your teeth into a steak, and they stay there.
12. You turn out the light for economic reasons rather than for romantic reasons.

BOW-WOW

247.

Four guys are bragging about how smart their dogs are. The first works for Microsoft; he says that his dog is probably the smartest dog on the planet...can actually do mathematical calculations. "His name is 'T-Square,'" the guy says. He tells the dog to go to the blackboard and draw a square, a circle and a triangle, which he does with no sweat.

The second guy is a Ford worker and says that his dog is even smarter. He is called "Slide Rule". His owner tells him to go get a dozen cookies and divide them into four piles of three, which he does with no problem.

The AT&T worker acknowledges that that was a pretty good trick, but says that his dog "Measure" is even smarter. He instructs his dog to go get a quart of milk and pour 7 ounces into a 10 ounce glass, which he does accurately and with dispatch.

All three agree that all of their dogs are exceptionally smart and turn to the fourth guy, a Civil Service worker, and ask him, "What can your dog do?" The latter says, "My dog's name is 'Coffee Break'" and tells his dog, "Show them your stuff!"

"Coffee Break" goes over, eats the cookies, drinks the milk and screws the other three dogs, claims that he injured his back, files for Worker's Compensation and leaves for home on sick leave.

ODE TO THE FOUR-LETTER WORD

248.

Banish the use of the four-letter word,
Whose meaning in never obscure.
The Angles and Saxons, those bawdy old birds
Were vulgar, obscene and impure.
But cherish the use of the weasling phrase
That never says quite that you mean.
You'd better be known for your hypocrite ways
Than vulgar, impure and obscene.

When nature is calling, plain speaking it out,
When ladies, God bless 'em, are milling about,
You may wee-wee, make water or empty the glass,
You may powder you nose…even Johnnie may pass,
Shake dew off your lily, see a man 'bout a dog;
When everyone's soused, it's condensing the fog.
But please do remember, if you would know bliss,
That it's only in Shakespeare that characters p—s!

A woman has bosoms, a bust or a breast,
The lily-white swellings that bulge 'neath her vest;
They are towers of ivory, sheaves of new wheat;
In moments of passion, ripe apples to eat.
You may speak of her nipples as fingers of fire
With hardly a question of raising her ire,
But by Rabelais' beard, she will throw several fits,
If you speak of them roundly as good honest t—s!

It's a cavern of joy you are thinking of now,
A warm tender field awaiting the plow.
It's a quivering pigeon caressing your hand,
Or the national anthem; it makes us all stand.
Or perhaps it's a flower, a grotto, a well,
The hope of the world, or a velvety hell,
But friend heed this warning, beware the affront
Of apeing the Saxon; don't call it a c—t!

So banish the words that Elizabeth used
When she was queen on her throne.
The modern maid's honor is easily bruised
By the four-letter words all alone.
Let your morals be loose as a commissioner's vest
If your language is always obscure;
Today not the act but the word is the test
Of the vulgar, obscene and impure.

PROCLIVITIES

249.
    Picture, if you will…a guy and a girl seated at a bar in a classy cocktail lounge. She is a knockout, so he says, "Buy you a drink?" She says, "Fine, but before you carry this further, I think I should let you know that I'm a lesbian." The guy says, "What difference does that make?" She says, "Do you see that girl

at the other end of the bar…the great-looking blonde? Well, being a lesbian I'd like to take her to my apartment, strip her down to her bare skin, place her on the bed and…(here she describes in some detail what she would then do with and to this girl)." At this the guy looks totally dejected, a lone tear sliding down one cheek. The girl says, "What's wrong?" He replies, "I think I'm a lesbian."

THE WARNING

250.

Picture, if you will…a kid who has just been discovered by his father in an act of self-abuse. Dad says, "You shouldn't do that sort of thing, Johnny, and if I ever catch you doing it again I'm liable to cut it off." The kid replies, "Girl next door had hers cut off…they tucked in the edges…looks pretty good!"

CAJUN TALE

251.

Thibedeau and his girl friend are on the way home from a social event in Sunset, LA. This is Cajun country. It is late in the evening and quite dark. He has to relieve himself, bladderwise, so he pulls over onto the shoulder and stops the car. He doesn't want to tell her what his problem is, so he tells his lady friend that he wants to check one of the tail lights on his vehicle and exits the car to accomplish what he has in mind. Well, he is standing there, hoo-hoo in hand spraying the stream back and forth in the ditch, when an indignant voice is heard to exclaim, "Hey, there, stop pissing on me!" Thib replies, "Watch your language, I got a lady here in the car!" The other quickly responds, "What you think I got down here in the ditch, a alligator?"

THE GRAFT

252.

A vet returning from the Vietnam war was checked into a VA hospital to see what could be done about his hoo-hoo having been shot off. Luckily for him they had a surgeon on staff that was able to compensate him for his loss by grafting to his stump six inches of an unborn baby elephant's trunk. As he was checking out of the hospital the doctor told him to report in 30 days how the grafting was going. He did as was asked and reported to the surgeon who had performed the delicate operation one month to the day later. The doctor asked how he was getting along and was there any problem or side effect that was evident. He answered, "It's great, Doc; it works very well and is much admired by the ladies. There is one thing that I guess you would call a side effect; it really bothers me at a cocktail party when they pass the peanuts!"

THE FAMILY GIFT

253.

Here we have a Vietnam vet who had returned from the war scene minus his hoo-hoo which was shot off in a firefight. They stopped the bleeding and sent him home post haste. When he arrived in his hometown the chief surgeon at the VA hospital called a conference of all of the male members of his patient's family. He told them that great strides had been made in the science of organ grafts and that the vet could be made whole if each of them were to contribute part of his hoo-hoo to the operation. With a conspicuous showing of family generosity and solidarity, each of the six of them agreed to do his part.

Well, the operation was eminently successful, and the donee of these magnanimous family gifts was able to lead a normal life. Well, in due time he got married, and of course he told his bride the wonderful story that allowed him to have a normal sex life with her.

When they returned from the honeymoon there was a family dinner, and the whole family was present. She addressed the donors very warmly, saying that their personal sacrifices were very much appreciated, "But", she said, "why did they have to put Grandpa's contribution in the middle?"

THE PRECAUTION

254.

In our town the gynecologist always wanted to have the husband present when he examined a woman's nether region. On this one occasion, as the woman and the man were leaving the examining room, the doctor took the man aside and said, "Boy, I've never seen a woman so nervous when being a examined." "Yeah," said the man, "Who was she?"

GOOD ADVICE

255.

A wise man once said, "If it flies, floats, rides on wheels, or f—ks, don't buy it; rent it.

DOMICILIARY REHABILITATION

256.

Down near Vergennes, Vermont a newly-arrived couple bought the old Hokey place. The real estate agent said that Olin Warren, who lived in the area could do any repairs they might want or need. So they set forth to find Olin Warren and encountered a man scything brush by the road. The following conversation ensued:

New Arrivals: "Do you happen to know Olin Warren?"

Man: "Yep, (Points to house up a hill a few hundred yards away.) Lives up thar."

N.A.: "Happen to know if he's home?"

Man: "Nope, he ain't ta home."

N.A.: "We're told that he'd be willing to do some repairs for us on the old Hokey place."

Man: "I be he."

ABOUT THE WEATHER

257.

Picture, if you will...two Vermont farmers meeting on a country road. One says, "Hi, Lem, d'ya think it'll rain?" The other replies, "Well if'n it don't, it'll be a long dry spell."

THE COUNTRY STORE

258.

Picture, if you will...a crossroads-country-store somewhere in New England. The proprietor is sittin' on the front porch arockin' and awhittlin'. An old regular customer comes up and says, "Hi, Jasper. Say, do ya have any of that thar breakfast cereal they're pushin' so much on tellyvision lately?"

"Nope," he replies, "Don't stock it no more; sold too fast."

NATIVE-AMERICAN WISDOM

259.

This chap is negotiating with a Native-American lady of the night. He asks how much, and she says, "$100." He replies, "$100? Why Manhattan cost only $24!" "Yes," she says, "But it just lies there."

FRENCH WEDDING NIGHT

260.

This is a story about a French bridegroom that was so exhausted by the elaborate wedding and reception, that he fell sound asleep the minute his feet hit the pillow.

INTERFAITH MARRIAGE

261.

A devout Catholic girl marries a Protestant fellow, and they set up housekeeping. One Sunday morning quite early, the wife gets up out of bed quietly and starts to get dressed. She puts on her bra, pantyhose and is just putting on her half slip when she notices a rather conspicuous bulge in the sheet where her husband is lying. She quickly gets undressed and slips under the sheet to enjoy one of the perks of married life. Her husband says, "I can't believe this;

you've never missed early Sunday mass since I have known you." She replies, "The Catholic Church is strong enough to stand forever, but for how long can you trust a Protestant prick?

THE MAINE MAN

262.

Up near Bangor, Maine, a man was hired to drive a widow lady. He was rather loquacious, and she didn't like the constant stream of random chatter, so she said, "You were hired to drive, not talk." When he submitted his bill at the end of the engagement there was an item that she did not expect: "Sass - $5.00" When she questioned the validity of the item, he said, "I don't often take sass, but when I do, I charge."

THE BURIAL

263.

Grandma died in a small town on the coast of Maine, and there wasn't any wood around to make a casket for her, so the family cinched her up snugly in an old sail. Her granddaughter was heard to chuckle as they lowered Grandma into the grave. She was scolded later by her mother, and she explained, "I know it was awful of me, but I couldn't help laughing at the thought of Grandma scudding through Hell in a close-reefed topsail."

BUILDING THE WALL

264.

Up there in rural Vermont a man was observed building a wall four feet wide and three feet high. Someone asked him why he was building such an odd-shaped wall...wider than it was high. Without looking up from his work, he said, "So iff'n it evah blows ovah it'll be hiah than it was befoah."

THE CURIOUS BRIDE

265.

New bride to priest: "Tell me, Father, is it all right to have intercourse just before you take communion?" Priest: "Certainly, my child, just so long as you don't block the aisle."

A GRAVE MATTER

266.

Mr. Johnson is looking over his backyard fence and notices that the little girl next door is digging a hole in the ground, so he asks her why she is digging the hole. She says, "My goldfish is dead, so I'm digging a grave for him." Mr. Johnson says, "I'm sorry you lost your goldfish, I know it must have meant a lot to you." "Yes," she says. "it did; I loved it." "Well," he says, "I think that's nice, burying him like that, but why are you digging such a big hole for a little goldfish, if I may ask?" "Because," she says, my goldfish is in your f—kin cat; that's why."

IMPENDING SEPARATION

267.

Riley arrives home late one evening after tossing a few at the pub with the boys. He sees a note from his wife on the dining room table which says, "The night before last you came home yesterday. Last night you came home this morning. If you come home tomorrow today, I'm going back to my parents tonight."

A STRANGE ORDER

268.

The madam at the fancy house asks a recently arrived stranger what sort of girl he desires. He says, "I want a fat lady with scraggly unkempt hair, a pockmarked face and varicose veins in her legs. I'm homesick."

PERFECT LOVER?

269.

The perfect lover has been defined as "A French man with a nine inch tongue who can breathe through his ears."

NO OBJECTIVE SIGNS

270.

A girl consults a doctor complaining of low-back pain. There are no objective signs that would explain this, so the doctor questions her and finds that her bowel movements are regular and she has a marvelous sex life preferring to do it "doggie style". The doctor says, "You might try changing it to the missionary style to see if that would alleviate your low-back pain." She replies that she doesn't like missionary style…her dog has bad breath.

TOOTHPICKS AND SUCH

271.

They say that French kissing is like a toothpick; you can use it on either end.

A 4-CYCLE ENGINE

272.

A guy is trying to explain to an intellectually-challenged young lady of his acquaintance how a 4-cycle engine works. He says that they call it a 4-cycle engine because there are four phases to its operation, namely, intake, compression, ignition and exhaust cycles. She doesn't seem to get it, so he says,

"Let's see if I can express it in terms with which you are more familiar: sucking, squeezing, banging and blowing."

THE SECRET OF A HAPPY MARRIAGE

273.

First man: "I can't get over how well you and your wife get along. Don't you ever have differences of opinion?"

His friend: "Oh, yes…very often."

F.M.: "And yet you seem to get over them very quickly."

H.F.: "Ah, that's the secret. I never tell her about them."

THE HEREAFTER

274.

Picture, if you will…a lady sitting out on her front porch, seemingly in a state of conspicuous meditation; her pastor approaches and says to her, "I can tell by the look on your face, Sister Eleanor, that you are thinking about 'the hereafter'." She replies, "No, as a matter of fact I wasn't, Reverend, but I do think about 'the hereafter' a good deal. I'll go upstairs to my bedroom, stand there a minute or so, and I'll say to myself, 'What am I here after?'"

DOOLEY'S GONE

275.

"I'm gonna miss old Dooley," says Pat, standing outside the funeral parlor. "Yeah, he was a gentleman all right; he always took off his hat before he beat up his wife.!"

GOOD READING

276.

An American is speaking with a Frenchman; he says, "My favorite novel is about a middle-aged Frenchman who has an affair with a 12-year-old." "Go on," says the Frenchman, "A 12-year-old what?"

SPACED OUT

277.

You ask, "Why no French astronauts?" Answer: "Who ever hard of a Frenchman going up?"

THE BREATHALYZER TEST, FRENCH STYLE

278.

An American chap is arrested in Paris for DUI and taken to the station for a breathalyzer test. The print-out appears, and the policeman reads it to himself, and then, shaking his head, he reads it aloud, "Veree disappointing, M'sieu…Chateau DuValier, 1987…rather thin…hasn't aged well."

TROUBLE IN THE BAR

279.

Dooley comes into the bar and says, "Quick, bartender, give me three double whiskies before the trouble starts." The bartender complies, and Dooley swiftly downs them, one after the other. The bartender observes this and says, "When does the trouble start?" Dooley answer, "Right about now; I can't pay for the whiskies."

DRINKING UNDER DURESS

280.

Finnegan, a bit loaded, is lurking in the shadows in an alley one evening, when a man walks by. He jumps out and accosts the man, gun in hand, and drags him into the alley. Then, taking a pint bottle of booze from his coat pocket, he points the gun at the man's head and says, "Here, take a good swig of this." Too terrified to resist, the man takes a healthy swallow and then exclaims, "Ugh! that stuff is terrible!!" "Yeah, I know," says Finnegan. Now you hold the gun on me and force me to drink some."

COURTROOM DRAMA

281.

Picture, if you will…a courtroom; a rape trial is in progress, and the D.A. is interrogating an eyewitness. After going through the preliminary questions that establish his having been there and seen that, the prosecutor says, "All right now, Mr. Russell, tell us what you observed."

"Well, what I saw," says the witness, "was that man over there (he points to the defendant) f—king the girl…" Here the Judge interrupts and says, "You can't say that in the courtroom." So, the witness says, "Well, as I was saying I was right there and saw him f—king the pants right off that girl…" Again the Judge interrupts the trial and says, "I told you that you can't say that here."

Again the witness tries to say what happened right there in front of him at the time in question, saying "I'm trying to tell you, Judge, that I saw that man f—king that girl." Again he was admonished by the Judge, so the witness, feeling quite frustrated, says, "His pants was down, his ass was bare; his balls were flying in the air. His you know what was you know where, and if that ain't f—king, I warn't there!"

IN THE BAR

282.

"Bartender, do you serve lawyers in here." "Sure", says the BT. "Okay, give me a bourbon on the rocks, and give my alligator a lawyer."

TWO MEN IN THE JOHN

283.

This man was standing there taking a pee, when he noticed that the man standing in front of the next urinal had an extremely long hoo-hoo. He remarked to the latter, "That's some long hoo-hoo you have there mister; it must be an organ of magnificent proportions when it's the state of erection!" "Well, to tell you the truth, mister", he responds, "I've never seen it in the state of erection; when I get a hardon it drains so much blood out of my system I always black out."

THE WEDDING RECEPTION

284.

Picture, if you will…a rather swanky wedding reception. One of the guests drinks too much and becomes rather obstreperous. The Wackenhut guards throw him out, but he sneaks back in and drinks even more, and he gets bodily ejected again. The bride says to her groom, "I don't think I know that man, dear, do you?" "Yes, as a matter of fact, I do. He's my first cousin twice-removed."

THE SECRETARY'S NEW BOSS

285.

One secretary asks another, "What's your new boss like?" She replies, "He's bigoted; he thinks that words can only be spelt one way."

DIFFERENCE BETWEEN LADY AND A DIPLOMAT

286.

If a diplomat says "Yes", that means "Maybe." If he says, "Maybe", that means, "No". If he says, "No.", he's no diplomat.

If a lady says, "No" that means "Maybe". If she says "Maybe" that means "Yes". If she "yes", she's no lady.

THE BIRTHDAY PRESENT

287.

One guy: "What did you give your son for his birthday?"

Other guy: "This year I gave him a sweater; last year I gave him a moaner and groaner."

SENIOR SEX AND RELIGION

288.

You know you're getting old when your wife gives up sex for Lent, and you find out on Good Friday.

THE ANIMAL ACTIVIST

289.

Picture, if you will...two ladies meeting on the street; one is enrobed very elegantly in a full-length mink coat. The other is somewhat of an animal activist; she disapproves of fur coats and doesn't mind letting people know about her feeling in this regard and is, as a matter fact, aggressively pushy on the subject. She has accosted the lady in the fur coat and says, in support of her viewpoint, rather loudly, "Do you know how many animals they killed to make that coat you're wearing; do you??" "No, I don't, my dear. Do *you* know how many animals I had to f—k to get this coat?!"

THE ENGLISH COUPLE AND THE ALTERED ROUTINE

290.

Picture, if you will...an English couple making love; she has just given him head and has committed his ejaculate to a handy kleenex. He says, "Well, my deah, I guess the honeymoon is ovah; you used to swallow the stuff." She replies, "It's not that, Reggie, eckchually it's my diet; they tell me that it is about 200 calories, and, frankly, my dear, I'd rawthah have a good glahss of wine!"

THE PICKY CANNIBALS

291.

Picture, if you will...a tribe of cannibals; they have just terminated a bunch of missionaries, and among other goodies they have acquired in the process of capturing their dinner is a case of Pepsi Cola which they enjoy with the dinner. At the conclusion of this meal it was noted that they had eaten all of the component parts of the missionaries except for their "things" because, as everyone knows, "Things" go better with coke.

THE BEST LOVERS

292.

Picture, if you will...a 747 that has just taken off; occupying adjacent seats in row 2, first class, are a very elegantly attired and beauteous lady in her early thirties and a well-groomed and attractive young man of about 40. She opens the conversation by introducing herself and adding that she is the incoming president of an organization known as N.A.N. Without a pause she reveals that the letters stand for National Association of Nymphomaniacs. He says, "Well, I bet you know a lot about sex, don't you, Madame President?" "Yes I do; our organization has many members, and we all have the benefit of each other's experiences in the field. One statistic that most people seem to be interested in is the question of what kind of men make the best lovers. And it may surprise you to learn that the consensus is that Native American Indian men are number one and Jewish men are number two. By the way, you have neglected to introduce yourself." To this the gentleman in question says, "Oh, I'm sorry; please forgive me; you are seated next to Geronomi Schwartz."

THE SEX TOY STORE

293.

Picture, if you will…a sex shop. On the particular day with which we are concerned the proprietor is talking to a friend of his on the premises of this little boutique. He says, to his friend, "Say, George, I've got to run over to the post office; can you take over? Things are pretty quiet." His friend readily acquiesces, and the prop leaves. When he returns, he asks whether there had been action, and his friend says, "Not much activity, but I sold some dildoes; I sold a white one to a black girl for 30 bucks, a black one to a white girl for 30 bucks and the big plaid one to a Polish girl for 50 bucks." "Fantastic! 30 bucks a piece for the white one and the black one is good, but getting 50 bucks from the Polack for my thermos bottle is amazing."

THE BIG DATE

294.

Two elderly men living at the nursing home are talking. Sam says to Ben, "I have a hot date tonight with two twenty-year-old chicks."

Ben says, "Do you have any VIAGRA?" Sam shakes his head "No!", so Ben hands him two VIAGRA and says, "Take both of them, and let me know what happens tomorrow."

The next day, Ben sees Sam with his arm in a sling. He says, "What happened last night?" And Sam replies, "The girls never showed up!"

DEFINITION

295.

The new Websters defines "Black Power" as a tall glass of prune juice.

SOME TYPES YOU MIGHT MEET IN THE MEN'S ROOM

296.
1. SOCIABLE…Joins friends in a piss whether he has to go or not.
2. TIMID…Cannot piss if someone is watching, flushes urinal and comes back later.
3. CROSS-EYED…Looks into next urinal to see how the other guy is hung.

4. INDIFFERENT...All urinals are in use; pisses in the sink.
5. CLEVER...No hands, fixes tie, looks around, pisses on the floor.
6. FRIVOLOUS...Plays stream up, down and across urinal, tries to hit fly or bug.
7. CHILDISH...Pisses directly in bottom of urinal; likes to see bubbles.
8. SNEAKY...Passes gas silently while pissing, acts very innocent, walks away feeling sure that the man next to him will get blamed.
9. URGENT...Teeth are floating, is out of time, pisses in pants.
10. TOUGH...Bangs hoo-hoo on side of urinal to get the last drop.
11. OBESE...Backs up, takes a blind shot at urinal; pisses on shoe.
12. EFFICIENT...Has waited until he has to crap, so does both.
13. DRUNK...Holds left thumb in right hand, pisses in pants.
14. DISGRUNTLED...Stands for awhile, gives up, walks away.
15. CONCEITED...Holds three-inch hoo-hoo like a baseball bat.
16. PATIENT...Stands there for a long time, reads paper with free hand.

<u>GLOSSARY OF MEDICAL TERMS FOR BUDDING DOCTORS</u>

297.

ARTERY:	The study of paintings.
BARIUM:	What they do when a patient dies.
BOWEL:	a, e, i, o, u.
CAUTERIZE:	Made contact with her.
D. & C.:	Our nation's capital.
DILATE:	To live long.
FESTER:	Quicker.
GENITAL:	Non-Jewish person.
IMPOTENT:	Distinguished, well-known.
LABOR PAIN:	Getting hurt at work.
MORBID:	A higher offer.
NITRATES:	Cheaper than day rates.
OUTPATIENT:	Someone who has fainted.
NODE:	Was aware of.
POSTOPERATIVE:	A letter carrier.
RECOVERY ROOM:	A place that does upholstery.
RECTUM:	Damn near killed him.
TERMINAL ILLNESS:	Getting sick at the airport.
TUMOR:	Plus two.
URINE:	Antonym of you're out.
VEIN:	Conceited.

GOD THE ENGINEER

298.

The human body is referred to as "The Incredible Machine". Of course the engineer that designed this machine was a true genius. There was only one real goof in the design, namely, viz and to wit: He placed the playground adjacent to the sewage disposal facility.

THE FARMER WANTS A DEEVORCE

299.

A=Attorney
F=Farmer

A. Do you have grounds?
F. Yup; I've got 30 acres.
A. No; that's not what I mean. Do you have a case?
F. Nope, I got a John Deere. That's what I farm them 30 acres with.
A. No, no. You're not understanding me. Do you want to bring suit? Do you have a grudge?
F. Well, I have a suit in my closet. The grudge; that's where I keep my tractor, the John Deere.
A. We're not communicating. Let's talk about your wife; do you beat her up?
F. Nope, she gets up about 5:30, about the same time I do.
A. No, no! Is she a nagger?
F. No but the kid was; that's why I want a deevorce.

MODERN DAY LEXICON FOR BUSINESSMEN

300.

A COMPETIVE YEAR: Sales are down.

OPERATIONS AUDITS: Cost chopping, usually followed by mass downsizing.

RESTRUCTURING: Deleting the deadwood from the Executive Suite.

UNDERGOING A CAREER ADJUSTMENT: The condition of an executive who has just been fired; often referred to as having been "dehired" or "outplaced".

COMMITMENT TO SOCIALLY DESIRED OBJECTIVES: A vow taken by company officials after losing a series of consumer suits or paying fines for pollution, or both.

MULTI-MARKET, MASS-CONSUMER, TECHNOLOGICALLY-ORIENTED, UNIFIED-MANAGEMENT COMPANY: A conglomerate.

CO-ORDINATOR: A guy who has a desk between two expediters.

CONSULTANT: Any ordinary guy more than 50 miles from home.

ACTIVATE: To add more names to the memo.

DECENTRALIZING THE COMPANY: The anti-trust people are threatening to step in.

PROGRAMMED POWER SHEDDING: The electricity will be shut off.

DEPARTMENT OF SPECIAL MARKETS: The office headed by the firm's showcase African-American executive, who is occasionally asked for advice on selling to blacks.

DEMOGRAPHIC SKEW: A goof made by the marketing researchers that make a new product all but unsalable.

MAJOR-LEVERAGE IMPACT: The profit expected to be made from a project, an estimate usually accompanied by a number of "results-oriented hypotheses" to prove that the idea is "viable".

SUBOPTIMAL COST PROFILE: The project costs too much. At this point the project has reached a "mature configuration" and is promptly dropped, along with the originator of the project.

ABIDING FAITH IN AMERICAN YOUTH: Sooner or later they will come to their senses.

GOVERNMENT COMMUNICATION CODE

301.

The premise is that the public is entitled to know what government officials mean when they use certain words and phrases; here are some that are typical and oft-used.

EXPEDITE: To confound confusion with commotion.

UNDER CONSIDERATION: Never heard of it.

UNDER ACTIVE CONSIDERATION: Someone is looking in the files for it.

RELIABLE SOURCE: The guy you just met.

INFORMED SOURCE: The guy who told the guy you just met.

UNIMPEACHABLE SOURCE: The guy who started the rumor in the first place.

NOTE AND INITIAL: Let's spread the responsibility for this one.

WE ARE MAKING A SURVEY: We need more time to think of an answer.

A FEW WAYS TO COPE WITH STRESS

302.

1. Use your MasterCard to pay your Visa, and vice versa.
2. Pop some popcorn without putting the lid on.
3. Push miniature marshmallows up your nose and sneeze them out. See how many you can do at a time.
4. Fill out your IRS Form 1040 using Roman Numerals.
5. When someone tells you to have a nice day, tell them you have other plans.
6. Leaf through National Geographic and draw underwear on the natives.

7. Dance naked in front of your pets.
8. Buy an issue of Hustler and send it to your boss's wife.
9. Do your correspondence in binary code.
10. Braid the hairs in both nostrils.
11. Sit naked on a shelled hardboiled egg.
12. Drive to work in reverse.
13. Pay the power company in pennies.
14. Write a short story using alphabet soup.
15. Bill your doctor for time spent in his waiting room.
16. Read the dictionary upside down and look for secret messages.
17. Replace the filling of a Twinkie with ketchup and put it back it the wrapper.
18. Buy a package of condoms, ask the cashier where the fitting room is, and ask for help.
19. Polish your car with ear wax.
20. Write "OUT TO LUNCH" on your forehead with a magic marker.

THREE FORMS OF CONTRACEPTION

303.

Withdrawal, douches and condoms. None is completely reliable. One is a pull-out, one is a washout and the third is a blowout.

SEEKING INFORMATION

304.

Picture, if you will...a neophyte skydiver. It's his first jump. He leaves the plane at 15,000 feet and freefalls to 5,000 feet. He pulls the ripcord and nothing happens; he tries again with no result. Just then he sees this woman wearing an apron coming up from below, shooting toward the heavens very rapidly. In his frustration he yells, "Know anything about parachutes?" She yells back, "No! Do you know anything about gas stoves?"

STREAKING

305.

We are told that what touched off the streaking craze of the sixties was when some poor devil reached for the Preparation H and by mistake picked up the Ben-Gay.

SPECIAL EFFECT

306.

The latest drink is called bourbon renewal. A couple sips and the whole neighborhood looks better.

EXCUSES FOR FALLING ASLEEP AT WORK

307.
1. This is just a 15-minute power nap like they encouraged in that time-management course you sent me to.
2. They told me at the blood bank that this might happen.
3. Wow! I must have left the top off the liquid paper…
4. I wasn't sleeping. I was just meditating on the mission statement and envisioning a new paradigm.
5. This is one of the seven positive habits of the highly effective employee.
6. I was testing the keyboard for drool resistance.
7. This is making up for the six hours last night when I dreamed about work.
8. Someone must have put decaf in the wrong pot.
9. I wasn't sleeping; I was trying to pick up my contact lens without using my hands.
10. Damn! Why did you interrupt me? I had almost figured out a solution to our biggest problem.
11. I'm doing a Stress Level Elimination Exercise Program (SLEEP) that I learned at that seminar you sent me to last month.

EINSTEIN THE TEACHER

308.

Picture, if you will…a very fancy cocktail party in an elegant penthouse apartment overlooking Central Park in Manhattan. Albert Einstein of "E-equals-emcee-squared" fame is one of the notables in attendance, as is a conspicuously adorable-looking young blonde girl who has just downed her second martini (very dry). She approaches the eminent scientist in question and says, "Oh, Professor Einstein, you're probably my favorite celebrity; my name is Sally Weston, and I am really, really happy to be able to meet you! They tell me that you can convert practically anything into a mathematical equation. Is that true?" He replies, "Ya." She continues, "Anything? Really? How about a 'sniff'?" "Uh vot?", he says. "A 'sniff'; you know." (Here she gives with a substantial sniffing sound.) "Ya, I kin do ziss. (He takes from his coat pocket a pen and a pad of paper, opens it to a blank page and resumes his explanation) Two rectangles plus two arcs plus eight right angles plus two zeroes plus two right triangles equals one sniff, like ziss:"

$$2 \,\boxed{S}\; + 2\, \complement_S + 8\, |^{\underline{\,}} + 2\, 0's + 2\, \triangleright\!\!\!\angle = 1\ SNIFF$$

Sally then says, "Could you please show me how you worked that out, Professor Einstein; I was never very good at math." Professor Einstein happily complies with this request and says: "First you take the two rectangles, like ziss:

zen you add ze two arcs, two zeroes und eight right angles:

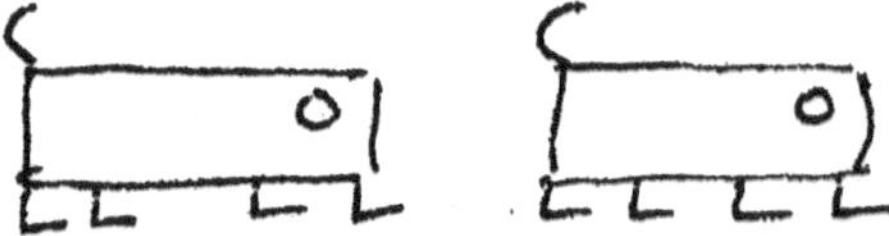

und finally two right triangles, und you haf your equation…"

FIND THE CULPRIT

309.

For this exercise you will need the cooperation of a naïve and ingenuous person of child-like simplicity, or someone who can fake those qualities, to help you in your presentation. You first draw three circles and pupiless eyes on a sheet of paper or a blackboard or whatever is available, thusly:

You then ask your assistant to draw in the pupils of the eyes so that the face on the left appears to be looking toward the one in the middle, the one on the right appears to be looking toward the one in the middle and the last appears to be looking upward, thusly:

Then, when this has been satisfactorily completed, you ask your helper to draw in the mouths of the one on the right and the one on the left so that they appear to be unhappy campers, and the mouth on the one in the middle so that he appears to be ecstatically happy, like so:

Then when this has been done you say, "Now this is the question: 'Which of the three passed gas in the lift?" (British for 'elevator'.)

SUBJECT CROSS-INDEX
(VOLUME CHOO)
References are to joke numbers

-T-

-U-

-V-

Vacations- 11, 29
Vegetables- 17
Ventriloquists- 112
Veterinarians- 34
Viagra- 116, 125, 294
Videos- 184
Virginity- 92, 121
Visitors- 120
Vulgarity- 10, 31, 248, 255, 266
Vulva- 144

-W-

Wagers- 25
Waitpersons- 1, 30
War- 165, 252, 253
Warnings- 144
Wealth- 12, 121
Weapons- 123, 280
Weather- 29, 174
Weddings- 92, 260, 284
Well- 132
What d'a get?- 48, 108, 219
Widowed persons- 77, 112, 163, 209, 275
Wine- 30, 221, 290
Winners- 94
Wisdom- 83, 84, 106
Woman/women- 31, 43, 45, 64, 75, 109, 134, 164, 185, 192, 238, 240, 242, 249, 251, 262, 274, 286, 289, 304
Word usage- 18, 19, 65, 107, 194, 203, 222, 286, 289, 297, 300, 301, 306
Wrestling- 94
Writers- 33

-Z-

Zoos- 80

ABOUT THE AUTHOR

Richard R. Booth, an attorney, is co-founder and Executive Director of *The Society of Loquacious Verbosities* and a contributor to the *South Miami Times, The Coconut Grove Times* and *The Brickell Post* (Miami, Florida) as The Sentient Scrutator and Just Joking. He is a former lecturer at the University of Miami on *The Art of Effective Speech,* and a calligrapher specializing in Olde English Illuminated Manuscripting (The Last of the Great Monks). Booth is a former federal prosecutor and a former judge. He was a World War II fighter pilot (P-38, *Lightning* and P-51, *Mustang* type aircraft) with the Ninth Air Force, European Theater, having flown fifty combat sorties.